Classic Pathfinder 2

Challenging classes

Classic
PATHFINDER

Classic
PATHFINDER

2

Challenging classes:
focus on pupil behaviour

JENIFER ALISON
& SUSAN HALLIWELL

CiLT
Centre for Information
on Language Teaching and Research

This compilation first published 2002 by the Centre for Information on Language Teaching and Research (CILT), 20 Bedfordbury, London WC2N 4LB

This compilation copyright © CILT 2002

Not bothered? Motivating reluctant language learners in Key Stage 4 first published 1993; second edition 2002; © CILT 1993, 2002

Yes – but will they behave? Managing the interactive classroom first published 1991; revised reprint 2002; © CILT 1991, 2002

Illustrations by Caroline Mortlock

ISBN 1 904243 05 3

A catalogue record for this book is available from the British Library

Printed in Great Britain by Cromwell Press Ltd

CILT Publications are available from: **Central Books,** 99 Wallis Rd, London E9 5LN. Tel: 0845 458 9910. Fax: 0845 458 9912. Book trade representation (UK and Ireland): **Broadcast Book Services,** Charter House, 27a London Rd, Croydon CR0 2RE. Tel: 020 8681 8949. Fax: 020 8688 0615.

Contents

Foreword

There have been many changes and developments in the teaching of Modern Foreign Languages since Susan Halliwell's and Jenifer Alison's original *Pathfinders* were written. More young people of all abilities are now studying foreign languages up to the age of 16 and the emphasis on communicative competence is seen as the norm rather than the exception in most classrooms. The National Curriculum for MFL puts the development of language-learning skills and learner independence at the heart of its programme of study. However, the complex issues of how to manage the classroom in order to achieve this continue to promote thought and discussion among MFL teachers.

Teachers want their pupils to develop confidence and competence in using the foreign language. They also want their pupils to develop fluency and accuracy and, at the same time, enjoy learning the foreign language. This commitment to making the learning of the foreign language a stimulating and rewarding experience for all pupils presents challenges and opportunities for even the most experienced teachers. It can be particularly challenging when our classes have a high proportion of reluctant, sometimes disruptive learners who are difficult to motivate.

In this *Classic Pathfinder* we are able to bring together strategies from both Jenifer Alison's and Susan Halliwell's work with a wide range of experienced teachers, trainee teachers and pupils. The title, 'Challenging classes', can be understood in two ways. 'Challenging' could be an adjective, meaning 'difficult to teach', or a verb, meaning that we make sure that every pupil in our class is suitably challenged. This book, which has grown from the *Pathfinders: Not bothered? Motivating reluctant learners in Key Stage 4* and *Yes – but will they behave? Managing the interactive classroom*, attempts to address both adjective and verb. It is indeed written very much in the spirit of the statement on 'Inclusion' in the National Curriculum for Modern Foreign Languages (Key Stages 3–4, p3):

> *'An entitlement to learning must be an entitlement to all pupils. This National Curriculum includes for the first time a detailed, overarching statement on inclusion which makes clear the principles schools must follow in their teaching right across the curriculum, to ensure that all pupils have the chance to succeed, whatever their individual needs and the potential barriers to their learning may be.'*

Jenifer Alison's experiences with the Year 10 in *Not bothered?* act as a springboard for Part 1, where approaches and strategies to cater for the characteristics and needs of disaffected students are distilled into seven ingredients for motivation. The wealth of tried-and-tested activities demonstrated in Chapters 4 to 9 (only four of the original *Pathfinder* activities have been retained) demonstrate how we can inject these ingredients into our teaching and classroom management. We read how we can create contexts and roles which appeal to the maturity level of students in Years 9 and 10, plan lessons that allow for logical progression in real-life terms as well as language and skills, and incorporate opportunities for independent differentiated learning. In order to achieve communicative competence that will allow them to feel confident and rise to the challenge of speaking in the target language when confronted with new situations or native speakers students need to be taught practical strategies, such as transferring language from one context to another, using a dictionary and other resources to find out new language. Jenifer Alison gives us ideas on how we can do this with challenging classes, which include students with learning difficulties. The overall aim is to ensure that all learners are included in projects and activities and feel valued and challenged and successful.

Parts One and Two complement each other perfectly. It is of course extremely sad that since writing *Yes – but will they behave?* Susan Halliwell has died. Her influence on generations of language teachers is great and her ability to analyse what actually makes pupils want to learn foreign languages and participate in classroom activities that will support their learning remains as accurate today as when the original *Pathfinder* was written. Susan was able to look in detail at the structures of Modern Languages lessons and devise strategies that would allow for the best possible use of teacher and pupil time. New influences on Modern Languages teaching, such as the **National Literacy Strategy** and **the Key Stage 3 Strategy** require us to look again at how we use the time that is available to us. Schools organise their MFL curriculum in a variety of ways: the length of individual lessons varies, the frequency of lessons is different from school to school, the time available for teaching the subject is also different; and yet pupils still have to reach appropriate National Curriculum levels and cover the programme of study. Susan Halliwell's descriptions and analysis of 'stir and settle' activities provide teachers with a repertoire of ideas on which to base starters and plenary sessions while maintaining a purposeful and manageable classroom atmosphere.

There is a wide range of good practice on which to draw when talking about effective MFL teaching. It is both significant and reassuring that HMI findings draw attention to the fact that 'one feature of good departments is that they are not afraid to state and act upon the obvious and that consistently successful teaching and learning are founded on getting simple things right, such as providing appropriate reinforcement in oral work or keeping clear records. The objectives of lessons are made explicit to pupils, stated clearly at the beginning of lessons and recapped at appropriate points' (Alan Dobson, HMI retired). These issues permeate the approaches to planning and teaching MFL lessons that feature in *Challenging classes* and we hope will provide teachers with a wide range of strategies that allow all pupils to feel included and valued in MFL lessons.

Carmel O'Hagan
Language Teaching Adviser, CILT

Part 1

Not bothered?

Motivating reluctant language learners in Key Stage 4

Acknowledgements

The original edition of *Not bothered?* and this version could not have been written without the generosity of teachers in North Lancashire and Cumbria who welcomed me in their schools, allowed me to teach their classes and were a great source of support and advice. Thanks also to the many teachers, who during workshops and conferences all over Britain so readily shared their ideas and experiences; to Claudine Domps, colleague and friend who supplied the French story for Chaotic listening (p37); to Steven Fawkes, BBC Education Officer (previously advisory teacher for Durham), James Burch, Principal Lecturer St Martin's College and Michelle Gibbins, Head of Department at Up Holland High School, who all gave me enormous support with the writing of the first edition.

In the preparation of this Classic Pathfinder I would like to thank specifically: Alison Bolt and the Modern Languages department at Parkview School, Barrow, whose policy of colour-coding mark books formed the basis of the differentiated zones (p23); Anna Downey (Lincoln Christ's Hospital School) and Barbara Bettsworth (Garstang High School) for their contributions to the activities for practising language; to Richard Walker (Alfred Barrow School) and Isabelle Mauboussin (Carr Hill School) for their contribution to the practical research upon which the conclusion is based. Finally, I would like to thank Chris Doyle, Deputy Head and French teacher at the Alfred Barrow School and her colleague Maureen Casey, Head of Modern Languages, who were also an on-going source of encouragement and inspiration, especially in the areas of Behaviour Management and Inclusion.

* Introduction

Think about the most challenging class you teach. Would it be a lower set, or a very mixed-ability Year 9 or Year 10 class? Would there be a mixture of willing, and reluctant and disruptive learners, where the latter dominate? Does this class take up what seems a disproportionate amount of your thinking and preparation time? Are the students in your mind in the early hours of the morning, as you puzzle out what motivates them and what you can try next? Do you have to wind yourself up before the lesson? Do the reluctant and disruptive learners dominate those who want to learn? Are your students perhaps happy just to sit and write, unwilling for you to disturb them by asking them to perform tasks that involve interaction in the foreign language? Does this class sometimes leave you feeling totally at a loss, depressed, de-skilled and inadequate by the end of the lesson?

I have had all of these experiences over the years with, in staff-room terms, 'difficult' classes. While working as a teacher trainer I 'borrowed' classes to teach on a regular basis. There were two reasons why I chose classes in the lower band of either Year 9 or Year 10. Firstly, I wanted to find out what made them tick and, secondly, teachers seemed very willing to relinquish them for a while. Each time, I taught them for a year. In doing this, I discovered that the problems above are more acute when the teacher is new to a school or class, because the students we are talking about find it hard to readily accept and trust a new teacher. It takes a lot of work on our part to build up a feeling of mutual liking and respect. These challenging classes, however, gave me great satisfaction when I tried strategies and approaches that did succeed in capturing their interest, and in doing so motivated them to learn. I also realised, that these approaches were, in fact, highly effective in other classes regardless of the ability level of the students within them.

This book is divided into nine chapters. Chapters 1–2 set the scene and are illustrated by examples from the first class I borrowed in a large local comprehensive, which I taught for a year while working as an advisory teacher for Lancashire. This class was the lowest set in Year 10 in a school with a 'Languages for all' policy. I refer to them in this book simply as 'Year 10'. We took a vocational approach, basing the language-learning programme on catering for foreign visitors to their town. This ran alongside their GCSE programme. They all achieved a GCSE grade in the end. Chapter 3 distils these experiences into ingredients for motivation. The subsequent chapters comprise a collection of ideas for contexts and roles followed by language-learning activities, which have all been tried and tested in classes similar to Year 10. Most of these activities move from whole class into individual, pair and group work. The emphasis here is on creating an inclusive classroom through independent and differentiated learning. The Conclusion addresses the question, 'What if none of this works with my class?', and the particularly unnerving experience of being new to such a class – and perhaps to the school as well. Challenging classes and students can put up a barrier which seems impossible for the teacher to break down. We look here at how we can find ways to break down those barriers without compromising good practice in MFL teaching.

1 Taking a closer look at our students

Think about your most challenging class for a second or two and jot down all the words that would best describe them.

Now look below. Compare your list with this one, compiled from teachers' contributions during INSET sessions.

Bored	Crude	Tired	Touchy
Careless	Resentful	Won't learn	Jealous
Forgetful	Aggressive	Untidy	Just want to write
Fidgety	Absent	Noisy	Can't concentrate
Lazy	Late	Inattentive	Don't do homework
Different from morning to afternoon, from one day to the next			

The Year 10 class I taught would answer to many of the descriptions above. I visited their school twice a week for a year just to teach them. Below I will describe in more detail how the students were, especially at the beginning. My dilemma was that they did not **all** fit the descriptions in the table above. Some were keen to progress and others were quiet and so often taken over by those who seemed to take it in turns to disrupt proceedings. Often they drifted late into the lessons, sometimes half asleep, sometimes in a dreadful mood. It was difficult to predict how they would react from one day to the next, from morning to afternoon, even from one lesson to the next. They were 'untogether', very 'physical' and generally 'not bothered'.

These 'Not Bothereds' would punctuate the lessons with noisy, impulsive behaviour. They would sit untidily in irregular positions. For no apparent reason they would get up and walk around or 'fix' the blinds, or even bang their heads against the desk or wall. They would push, shove and even lift chairs and tables, bang them with their fists and kick them. They often felt the need to hurl their bags and to shout across the room. The extract overleaf illustrates their impulsive highly physical reactions. (The names are fictitious.)

'You don't need to bring your bag!' I said to Darren as we were leaving the classroom to go on a visit to a local hotel. 'You don't need that!' repeated his friend, Scott, as he pulled it from his shoulder and hurled it back into the room spilling the contents on to the floor.

They were suspicious and jealous of each other and vied for attention – yet at the same time seemed to be totally ignoring me! Of course they were not all like this all of the time, but enough of them were at any one time to make it very difficult to speak to the class as a group.

As we got to know each other better, I discovered that many of them suffered from a deep sense of failure and felt extremely insecure in their relationships either at home or at school, or both. They experienced difficulty in expressing themselves in the foreign language and were frightened of revealing what they felt were their inadequacies. So, to protect their sensitive egos, they would attempt to divert my attention by covering all this up with noisy, disruptive behaviour, brushing off any reaction I made with 'I'm just **not bothered**, am I?' It seemed that if they couldn't gain status with the class and with me through achievement, then they would seek another way to be admired, by showing off their skills in disruption.

With 24 years of experience in teaching behind me, I underwent a very sharp learning curve over the time I spent with Year 10. The extract below shows one aspect of this. Ryan was an extremely disruptive influence and I am ashamed to admit that I was relieved one day to note his absence. I had the whole class working well, when he burst in. Read the extract below. Where did I go wrong?

Ryan burst in.
His friend banged the desk in welcome.
'Why are you late?' I said.
He'd slept in.
I told him what to do.
More desk banging from his friend.
I got cross.
Ryan was rude.
I complained.
He said he didn't know what he'd said.
He grumbled as he went to his seat, said he wasn't bothered.
He settled down to copy the work from his friend.

Had I shown my disappointment as he came through the door? Did I cause the negative response? Would it have made a difference, had I greeted him with, 'Good morning, Ryan, sit down and I'll come to see you in a moment'? Perhaps given him a smile as well? I may not have stopped the desk banging but might have retained the positive atmosphere we had been enjoying.

The approaches and strategies we consider in the next chapter originate from work with this class and have been developed through working with other classes since, together with many discussions with teachers around the country.

2 General approaches and strategies for motivating challenging classes

In our approach to our students we have two main obstacles to overcome. They resent being thought of as schoolchildren and they resent having to be in the classroom. Each of them wants to be treated as an adult person in his or her own right, but often doesn't know how to go about it in the school environment.

It does help if we can consider our students as adults. It also helps to delve beneath the off-putting behaviour of some to discover the reasons for it. When we do this, we find that their needs are indeed very similar to our own. Below is a list compiled from teacher responses during several INSET sessions to the questions, 'When do you switch off?' and, 'When do you, as an adult, feel motivated?'. How do you identify with the eight reasons for disaffection and the eight reasons for motivation?

Disaffection	Motivation
We switch off when:	**We are motivated when:**
1 We do not understand what is going on – it is not explained clearly.	1 There is mutual trust and respect in our working relationships.
2 It is boring, too hard, inaccessible, irrelevant.	2 We feel we have a useful contribution to make.
3 The speaker is going on for too long.	3 We feel valued and involved.
4 We cannot get involved.	4 We are able to participate and be busy.
5 There is no variety.	5 We feel safe – and not embarrassed by our inadequacies.
6 There is no stimulation.	6 We feel encouraged.
7 We feel we are being patronised.	7 We feel successful.
8 We don't feel valued.	8 We see the point in what we do.

Continuing on the assumption then, that our students have similar needs to us, we will take each one of the eight points which motivate us and see how we can take them into account in our general approach in the classroom.

 ENJOYING MUTUAL TRUST AND RESPECT IN OUR WORKING RELATIONSHIPS

Using the following strategies could help towards creating a feeling of trust and respect with our students.

Getting to know students better as individuals

Building up trust can be a very long process, full of ups and downs, and much of it is best achieved by finding opportunities to talk with our students individually. In talking about their interests, their hopes for the future, their problems we could:

• chat with individual students while the class is working independently (according to Jim McElwee the ICT room is a good place for this – see *Reflections on motivation,* Chapter 6, 'ICT makes it click');

• arrange to visit them in other subject areas, especially art, where the atmosphere often tends to be more informal;

• arrange visits or major projects involving working together during and perhaps outside lesson time, thus offering an opportunity for informal conversations;

• exchange a few friendly words as we encounter them on the stairs, in the corridor – or in the local supermarket;

• find out whether they are taking part in any extra-curricular activities, e.g. I discovered that three of the boys in Year 10 were in the school performance of the *Mikado* and that Ryan was part of an Irish dancing team – I didn't see the dancing but did watch the performance of the *Mikado,* and it was good to see this side of them.

Giving individual attention

As we get to know each student we can bring in material that we know is of interest to a particular individual and use that as a stimulus for language work. It could be a copy of *L'Equipe,* a magazine on cars, motorbikes, fashion, etc. We cannot do this all of the time, but the one time we do it will be remembered. (See *Boys' performance in Modern Foreign Languages,* pp42–43, para. 6.4, which points out the importance of interpersonal relationships; also p20, 4.4.1.)

When marking work, it shows our interest in them if we use their names in our comments. For example, *'Très bien, **Paul,** tu fais des progrès!'* This leads us to our next point.

Setting clear, manageable standards

Setting high standards for a piece of written work and acknowledging and recording achievement as soon as possible with a positive comment, marks or grades, can help to nurture individual relationships. This is because the student has tangible evidence that his or her efforts have been recognised and that we are taking his or her progress seriously.

In the extract below, Year 10 knew the criteria they were working towards for a piece of written work. Their interest in their results was both a surprise and an indication of their need for recognition and praise.

> *When I set up their first piece of written work I indicated they would receive a mark out of 15. That was, 10 for content plus 5 for presentation. I marked the work that evening and also added an asterisk for exceptionally well-presented work. When I gave the books back the next day, the first thing they did was to compare efforts and those who had a 'star' were pleased to broadcast the fact. Even at their age! I kept to this procedure!*

FEELING WE HAVE A USEFUL CONTRIBUTION TO MAKE

Keeping on the alert for positive contributions

This means constantly listening and watching, not only for misdemeanours, but also for the slightest manifestation of a positive contribution. It could just be a mumble to a friend and could easily go unnoticed in the general bustle of the lesson or in our concern to 'get through the work'. We need to pounce on it, praise it, try to turn it to the good somehow, even if it is incorrect or we struggle to see the relevance.

Turning less positive contributions to the good

We can even call students' bluff by diffusing the situation when they are trying to wind us up. We can do this by turning the situation back on to them as long as our response is seen as genuine and not sarcastic. If they make silly 'throw away' suggestions, we can prevail upon them to carry them out, as happened with Year 10 in the extract below.

> *When discussing what kind of items we could put in a tourist package for French people for the local tourist office, Carl and Liam suggested a pub-crawl. They were, I suppose, letting us know they knew about the things that mattered. However, they were taken up on their suggestion and asked to write out an itinerary on foot including four pubs. They found a map of the area and set to writing out the directions from one pub to another. Problems arose only when they couldn't agree where they all were!*

FEELING VALUED AND INVOLVED

As adults, we are far more interested in proceedings if we feel we have an important part to play. Equally our students are far more likely to work with us if we can make them feel part of the lesson. Creating situations where they might come forward to offer help allows them to demonstrate their strengths. We language teachers often work far too hard. Susan Halliwell's 'Superteach' (Part 2: *Yes – but will they behave?*, p82) comes to mind as we grapple with the flashcards, write on the OHP, mark up points in team games, ask questions and judge the answers. Many of these tasks could be taken over by the students, hence channelling their energy into positive involvement. Many teachers have experienced an increase in motivation once they are no longer the focus (see Chapter 3, p21). Students tend to behave better when being taught by their peers and the lesson becomes more theirs than ours. More on this approach is illustrated below with examples from my lessons with Year 10.

The **electronically minded person** could be responsible for the operation of the video recorder and television.

I'd recorded a part of their lesson on video and wanted to play it back on the video recorder. They were keen to see themselves, so, when I (on purpose) fumbled with the controls, Ryan came forward and took charge. We were adult to adult for that moment with him in the stronger position. Operating the video recorder (and camera) and television became his job every time this equipment was used.

The **bossy character** who talks incessantly is the ideal character to start off and run a group game.

We had a set of 'Teach and test' cards and the bossiest, most talkative person, James, was put in charge of testing the rest of a group of four. He immediately turned it into a kind of BBC quiz game and the group was absorbed – speaking lots of French – for at least ten minutes.

The **imaginative person** is invaluable. We can use the students' imaginations rather than exhaust our own repertoire of ways to make language learning fun!

During one lesson, I was 'slow feeding' acetate cut-outs on to the overhead projector to see who would be the first to decipher the messages on them. Chris offered to be the teacher and it was surprising how many different ways there were of putting a cut-out on the projector to make it a challenge for the others to read!

The students themselves created mimes to help them to remember the sounds of the alphabet. Their inventiveness was a revelation of the talent we have in our classrooms (see p44).

There may be someone who turns out to be particularly **thoughtful** and **protective** towards the weaker students. Remember him or her if someone new arrives in the class, if someone has been away ill and needs help to catch up, or if there is someone everyone tends to reject when it comes to grouping them.

The **tidy, meticulous person** could be in charge of the wall display.	*In a lesson in which the class could choose their activity, while James was running the BBC game with one group, another group was using the cassette recorder for a listening task, another writing up the letters to the places we wanted to visit while the last group was preparing the wall display. Display was a strength for Chris, the group leader.*
The **soapbox politician** could help with the organisation – and in fact run any main project the class may decide to take on.	*When we decided to produce a pack of materials for the local tourist office, we had a board meeting to discuss what form the pack should take, what the content should be and who should be responsible for which parts. The most difficult member of the group made a throw-away comment about needing a chairman. We called his bluff. He became chairman and did a most efficient job of organising the others, who listened to him far more attentively than to me. It came to light that he was involved in a council for Children in Care and therefore had experience in this field.*

HAVING A CHANCE TO PARTICIPATE – TO BE BUSY

Whole-class teaching or independent learning?

Students in challenging classes often have a wide variety of needs and catering for them all can be difficult in a whole-class situation. Attendance is also a problem. Students who have been away come in and don't understand what's going on, and this can lead to disruption of the whole class. Even if it doesn't, when we are at the front teaching the whole class we cannot give individual attention to those who need it.

Some things, of course, are more efficiently taught to the whole class. Some of the activities mentioned in Chapters 5–8 are very effective and enjoyable as whole-class activities, although they are designed specifically for groups and pairs. However it can be exhausting attempting to entertain and animate a whole group with a short concentration span. It is a golden opportunity for disrupting, even bringing the lesson to a complete halt. Mostly this is because some students have little chance or confidence to participate in this situation and lose the incentive to become involved.

FEELING SAFE AND NOT EMBARRASSED BY OUR INADEQUACIES

As adults we can find it difficult or embarrassing to speak in front of a large group of people for fear of losing face. There is no reason why our students should be any different. Indeed the problem is often more acute because they are at an age where they are very conscious of their image. We can avoid getting them into situations where they are made to look small in front of their contemporaries in the following ways:

- being aware of activities which demand students to be in the limelight unexpectedly. Making sure that they are confident with the task they have to perform before asking them to do it (see *Boys' performance in Modern Foreign Languages,* p27, para. 4.7.5, which asserts that whereas some boys love to be in the limelight, others have a distaste for speaking the foreign language in public and p32, 5.3 'Self image'. See also *Reflections on motivation,* p35, 'Self confidence');

- being aware of the temptation to pounce upon someone we know hasn't been listening, knowingly putting him or her into an embarrassing situation. We've proved our point but the effect has been negative;

- being careful which individual we ask to repeat again and again, in front of the class, a word he or she cannot pronounce. The whole situation is aggravating and can be acutely embarrassing for the victim;

- assessing progress on a formative, staged basis, with a view to building confidence. Continual failure is a major cause for 'throwing in the towel';

- allowing students to collaborate on tasks whenever appropriate. A straightforward listening comprehension, for example, can be a far more enjoyable and valuable exercise if tackled with the support of a friend. They learn to work as a team.

BEING ENCOURAGED

That small word of encouragement from our colleagues or from those in the higher echelons can have such a powerful effect on our self-esteem that we want to make even more effort to show what we can do! Many of our students have, by the time they reach Years 9 or 10, experienced years of failure and have developed a very low opinion of themselves. This can result in avoiding contributing to the lesson or taking a long time to begin tasks for fear of failure. Being sensitive in our treatment of efforts that they make can encourage further participation. Let us take the scenario where the teacher is asking questions to the whole class, inviting responses. The topic is, 'Where people work'. To the question, 'Where does the policeman work?' the teacher wants the answer, 'In the police station'.

Teacher	*Wo arbeitet der Polizist?*	Where does the policeman work?
Jane	*Polizstation.*	[Half German, half English answer]
Teacher	*Nein … Richard?*	No … Richard?
Richard	*In der Polizeiwache.*	In the police station.
Teacher	*Sehr gut Richard – das ist richtig.*	Very good, Richard, that is correct.

If we consider that Jane rarely pays attention to the lesson, her response at least shows interest and effort. To ensure she does not feel put down and to encourage further attempts, the teacher could treat it this way:

Teacher	*Vielen Dank, Jane, das ist eine Idee.*	Thank you Jane, that is an idea.
	Wer hat noch eine Idee? Richard?	Who has another idea? Richard?
Richard	*In der Polizeiwache.*	In the police station.

Teacher	*Sehr gut Richard – Jane?*	Very good Richard – Jane?
	Wo arbeitet der Polizist?	Where does the policeman work?
Jane	*In der Polizeiwache*	In the police station.
Teacher	*Fantastisch!*	Fantastic!

 ## FEELING SUCCESSFUL

'It's boring – can't do it – not bothered!' is a common refrain. We can bend over backwards explaining the advantages of speaking a different language but the students' outlook is often more to do with the fact that they like what they are good at. This has influenced options at the age of 14 just as much as the usefulness or love of the subject. We can encourage a gradual movement towards 'I'm good at that, it's OK' by engineering success and finding strategies to build up confidence. We need to convince students that they are not being assessed every time they open their mouths to speak and that the whole point of learning a different language is to be able to communicate with its speakers in the real world, where people use all kinds of coping strategies to help communication. This means adopting strategies to make the language they know go a long way! Year 10's GCSE successes offer evidence that the confidence they gained from this approach encouraged them to progressively replace these coping strategies with language. The following are three useful coping strategies (further reading on communication strategies can be found in *Reflections on motivation,* Chapter 7, 'Metacognition and motivation: learning to learn', p89, Terry Lamb and *Something to say?,* p14, Extract 9):

Selecting key words to convey the message

Once students realise that instead of grappling with, and trying to remember the intricacies of, long sentences it is permissible to select key words for what they really need to say, it can be a turning point. This was the case for Paul, who had been trying to ask, *'Vous habitez quelle ville?'* (Which town do you live in?). He then said, 'I don't need to say all of that, do I? I could just say, *"Quelle ville?"* (Which town?) couldn't I?' He had learned that, in the context of asking and noting the visitor's address, the listener would understand him and give the name of the town.

Transferring language from one situation to another

It can be enormously satisfying when this takes place. They might, for example, have learned to say 'I'm sorry' in the foreign language in the context of shopping, playing the role of the shopkeeper, and then use it when they arrive late to your class! They might have learned 'Can I help you?' in the context of working at a campsite and then use it when they offer to help you in the classroom. To do this is a skill which we need to teach them explicitly. In the following extract Ryan is asking for and noting an address. He gets stuck on the number – as they often do – and ingeniously transfers the expression *'Comment ça s'écrit?'* (How do you spell that?) to get the teacher to 'spell' out the number twenty in digits.

Ryan	*Quelle est votre adresse?*	
Teacher	*Numéro vingt ...*	[Ryan became very puzzled, searching the ceiling and the floor for clues, and then brought his coping strategies into play.]
Ryan	*Comment ça s'écrit?*	How do you spell that?
Teacher	*Deux et puis zéro.*	[He successfully wrote in the number twenty.]

Adopting non-verbal strategies when language fails

Using mime, pointing, showing or drawing pictures are all things which people do in real life situations when wishing to communicate meanings and the language fails. Some of our students will have found themselves in such situations and will have learned such skills, others will not and will need to be taught. As part of the simulation in the extract above, Ryan wanted to ask the number of my car.

Ryan	*Quel est le numéro de votre ...*	[Long pause followed by a grin and a mime of someone driving.]
Me	*Ah! Ma voiture?*	
Ryan	*Oui, voiture!*	[I then gave the number, which he noted correctly.]

Teaching students these strategies enables them to convey meanings in the foreign language. This success gives them the confidence to progress linguistically (see also *Boys' performance in Modern Foreign Languages,* p31, 5.2).

 SEEING A POINT IN WHAT WE DO

As adults we would not willingly do anything pointless unless we were enjoying it! These days, can we expect our students to carry out tasks just because we say so? Higher attaining students do what we ask of them more readily than lower attaining groups. This is because they tend to be more socially mature and ready to comply with our wishes. They tend also to be motivated by more distant goals, such as GCSE or the career they wish to follow. Lower attaining students often do not like to conform to classroom protocol **and** need a more immediate goal than GCSE. So, unless we can capture and keep their interest they can react by becoming very difficult to control. It is a question of discovering what is important to them and what is a valid purpose for an activity in their eyes. 'Seeing the point' permeates the ingredients for motivation in Chapter 3.

3   A recipe for motivation

Below is an attempt to distil the general approaches and strategies in Chapter 2 into seven basic ingredients for motivation.

Before reading the ingredients you might like to do two small tasks:

1   Think about your challenging class. At which points in the lesson have the students been most difficult? At which points have they been most motivated – even if only for three minutes? What were you doing and what were they doing?

2   Now look at the ingredients below. Were you including any of these during moments of increased motivation?

the seven main ingredients

1	Context

Are we:
- setting a scene which relates to the students' own experience?
- encouraging positive personal, social interaction?
- creating links with people outside the classroom?

2	Roles

Are we creating situations where students can develop or demonstrate:
- personal and social skills?
- communication skills?
- other work-related skills?
Could we create links with adults in local places of work, for example in a bar or restaurant, leisure centre, etc?

3	Challenge

Are the students challenged to:
- think?
- identify?
- guess?
- speculate?
- remember?

4	Differentiation

Do students have a chance to:
- decide which language they need to learn?
- contribute their own thoughts and feelings?
- demonstrate their strengths?

5	Purpose

Do the students have the chance to:
- listen, speak, read and write for a real purpose?
- understand why they are developing these skills?

6	Involvement and participation

Are we:
- getting students **doing?**
- letting students take charge of the lesson in a positive way?
Are the students:
- working independently?
- helping one another?
- teaching and testing one another?

7	Recognition of success

Do we:
- give positive feedback?
- set achievable targets?
- help students set their own targets?

CONTEXT

Keeping the lesson within a context

When we are under pressure to cover the content of the departmental scheme of work we can sometimes overlook the importance of motivating the class to learn effectively what we are covering, by creating contexts which relate to what is important to the students. It is helpful to have a coursebook that pitches the content to the interests of adolescents of today. Even then, we often need to give the tasks in them a twist to find a context to make that content more relevant to our students' own experience and what is important to them, and to appeal to their maturity.

Doing this encourages an active and personal response from the very start of a new topic. Take, for example, the topic, 'Town and surrounding area'. Many teachers choose to use the local area as a starting point, which allows the students to contribute their own knowledge and thoughts. Starting from a position of knowing something already and feeling they have some control over the lesson content can give them more confidence and motivation to contribute. Other topics lend themselves to fostering positive personal and social interaction. When we have created this context, we then need to keep the ensuing activities within it as far as possible.

ROLES

Allowing students to adopt roles with which they can identify

It helps to make language learning more meaningful if, having created a context relevant to the students, we can give them and ourselves roles within that context. To continue with the example of 'Town and surrounding area', how can we increase their motivation to talk about their own local area? Perhaps we could put them in a position to help a foreign tourist? We could be the tourist – even dress up as one. The students could be tourist officers or hotel receptionists. Taking on the role of helping someone can be motivating, because helping makes us feel good, perhaps because we are in the superior position here. One third of a Year 9 lower set interviewed after a project we did in 1998, based on helping French visitors to their local town, said that what they liked best was helping people.

A student could be:

• a tourist officer helping visitors find accommodation in town;
• a hotel receptionist booking someone in;
• an employee in a local shop;
• a railway employee helping foreign travellers;
• a publicity agent creating posters for the local hotel, etc.

Roles, settings and contexts based on catering for international visitors to our home town can fit well into most of the transactional GCSE topics. However, what about topics which come under 'Personal and social life'? Could we create the context here of two businessmen in the bar of a hotel making small talk? So many of the non-transactional topics students need to study for GCSE can come under the 'small talk' umbrella and the students can create their own settings for it. In doing this we are teaching them social and communication skills. After all, once they have bought a pint and ordered a meal for their business colleague they can't sit and stare at them while waiting for it to arrive, but need to make conversation. We perhaps take it for granted that they can do this – but in fact many have no experience of this social art.

CHALLENGE

Injecting challenge and incentive into activities

Injecting challenge into classroom activities means that the students can learn in spite of themselves.

Firstly, there are challenges similar to those which people enjoy in everyday life, such as scoring points in quiz games, winning races, etc. Here are some examples of how this can be reflected in the classroom:

- the first to identify, guess, speculate, for example in 'Grab a card' (see p38);
- challenge to remember language, for example in 'Win the card' (see p47);
- winning points over the teacher, as in 'Beat the teacher' (see p38), is invariably successful because it's human nature to enjoy catching out the boss.

Secondly, there are challenges related more directly to language learning. For example, getting the class to think, to arrive at the meaning of words, giving students ever-increasing clues, 'making the class struggle to arrive at meaning' (*Something to say?*, p22–29). We can also challenge individuals to progress by setting them targets to aim for, taking their different learning needs into account (see *National Curriculum for England: MFL,* p20, 'Inclusion').

DIFFERENTIATION

The main emphasis here is on inclusion. We are looking at practical ways in which we can meet the three principles for inclusion laid out in the National Curriculum.

1. Setting suitable learning challenges.
2. Responding to pupils' diverse learning needs.
3. Overcoming potential barriers to learning and assessment for individuals and groups of pupils.

In centring the learning on the students we open up our lessons to include differences in individual thoughts, interests and knowledge. Chapters 4 and 5 show practical ways of doing this. Students also bring different feelings in to the lesson. Are they confident, or lacking in self-esteem, easily embarrassed, etc? Chapter 5 shows how we can adapt activities to cater for these feelings by addressing learning needs. Chapters 4 and 9 give us ideas for activities and projects which are open-ended, allowing all students to perform at their own level. The two tables overleaf show how such activities can be differentiated. Table 1 shows a prepared and performed sketch and Table 2 a class information pack on the local area.

Table 1: Making and performing sketches

This assumes a class whose ability ranges from NC Levels 1–5 and covers ATs 2 and 4.

Levels 1–2	Level 3	Levels 4–5
• Make dialogues by filling in a matrix on a photocopy of what is on the OHP. • Use a list of words and phrases given at the bottom of the sheet. • Some students, who have extreme difficulty writing, might need to write over stencilled words and stick them in the gaps.	• Make dialogues using a matrix on the OHP. • Use the notes in their books to insert language into the gaps, e.g. **On peut** _visiter le musée_. 	• As for Level 3, but inserting other recycled language and experimenting with new, e.g. **On peut** _visiter le musée_. **Extra**: _C'est intéressant. J'adore les musées. Je suis allé(e) à Tullie House_ (museum in Carlisle) _la semaine dernière_ ..., etc.

Table 2: Preparing an information pack for the local tourist office for use by foreign visitors

This assumes a class whose ability ranges from NC Levels 1–5.

Level 1 / Level 2	Level 3	Level 4 / Level 5
Level 1 • Label a plan of the town **Level 2** • Copy phrases to label a poster of activities possible.	• Prepare a leaflet for the local tourist office. • Use notes to attempt sentences, short phrases. 	**Level 4** • Using notes and the grid, write three or four sentences about the local town. **Level 5** • Add what you did in the town last week.

Source: adapted from
Reflections on motivation,
Chapter 9, 'A vocational framework and its potential
to motivate, p112.

PURPOSE

Creating relevant contexts and roles, linking activities to the real world, for example the workplace and increasing challenge and incentive in day-to-day classroom activities, all help to give more purpose to language learning from the student's perspective. Also, if we can share with them the learning objectives behind the activities they are tackling, it should help them to identify better with what they are doing. We should 'enable our pupils to show interest in their work and think and learn for themselves', says OFSTED (see guidance in *Criteria for effective teaching and learning*). This is also reflected in the first element of four in the TLF strand, '... thinking skills linked to subject objectives'. (The TLF strand (Teaching and Learning in the Foundation Subjects) has as its main purpose to raise standards by encouraging good teaching, making teaching more effective and helping teachers to create the best conditions in which pupils can learn' (KS3 Pilot, 2/1/2001)). Let us take the example of a Listening task, targeting NC AT1, Level 4. Do our students know, that when we 'do' a Listening, the learning objective is to improve in the skill in 'identifying main points and some details'? Is that enough, or could we also give them a purpose for the activity itself? Are the results perhaps to be used as a stimulus for a spoken or written task – and what will the audience be for that?

INVOLVEMENT AND PARTICIPATION

Working in a whole-class situation with a challenging class is rather like sitting on a volcano. We feel we need to remain in charge, keeping students all together in order to maintain control. However, this can be counterproductive, leading to the situations below:

- Some students switch off after a very short time and make it practically impossible for us to speak and for the motivated students to work.
- Some students take a very long time to begin an activity and rarely finish it.
- Other students finish quickly and begin to chat – or worse.

Running teacher-led activities when we have very disruptive and disaffected students demanding nearly all of our attention and energy can make us feel, apart from exhausted, continually guilty that the undemanding students are being short-changed. There are two strategies that can help here:

1 Allowing students to be teacher clones, that is, to run the lesson for us at every opportunity. They feel the lesson belongs more to them and indeed often behave better towards their peers.

2 Using strategies such as timing the class, ('You have five minutes for this, then we'll move on to something else') encourages some to get on with tasks. However, this can be a problem for the student who genuinely needs more time – the frustration of never finishing and continually getting low, or no, marks is often a major cause of disaffection.

Increasing participation and involvement through independent learning

While working as a full class, even if we use the strategies above, individual students still have a limited chance to be included in the lesson and some will react by sabotaging it. Getting them to work independently and at their own pace has the potential to diffuse this situation. If we can provide tightly organised and monitored activities, with support and clear instructions, there is the chance that students should feel motivated to work in their own small units, or on their own. If there are those who do not, at least the focal point of the lesson has now switched from us to within smaller groups, working independently of one another. Therefore, if one group doesn't want to work, this is less likely to disrupt those wanting to get on. Once the class is busy on tasks independently of us, we notice that the atmosphere does become more relaxed. We can circulate and give the individual attention that is so badly needed. (See *Boys' performance in Modern Foreign Languages,* p18, para. 4.1.3, where Vee Harris is quoted as having found that 'there was a general concern with boys about the lack of independence offered in MFL classrooms in contrast to Maths or Physics'. See also *Reflections on motivation,* Chapter 8, pp96–97, 'A more adult way of working'.)

Ways to increase motivation to work independently

The more ingredients we can inject into the tasks we plan the more likely students are to get involved. For example, we can prevent eruptions by keeping students busy. They need to feel they are doing something. Susan Halliwell stresses the importance of physical as well as mental engagement in order to increase involvement and participation and gives us many ideas for activities that do this (see Part 2: *Yes – but will they behave?*). Here are some general strategies demonstrated in the activities in this book:

* injecting a tactile element into a task or activity. For example, in Chapter 8 there are suggestions for activities in which students are either handling cards, using a board game or noting scores. Noting things down makes them feel they are getting somewhere – they have evidence that they are working;

* allowing students to work collaboratively in pairs or in groups as much as possible.

Below is a three-stage pattern of working which has been successful. There is very little teacher input followed by a bank of tasks at the end allowing us to 'drip feed' instructions individually as students complete them. Look at Chapter 9 to see if you can detect this pattern.

1 A 'get-them-busy' start avoiding possible interruptions from latecomers.

2 The teacher-controlled part, which is planned to last for no longer than fifteen minutes, allowing us to ensure that students master the language they are going to need in order to tackle the bank of tasks and are given instructions for the first task.

3 The bank of tasks then allows students to work at their own pace, moving on to the next activity when ready. We drip feed the instructions for the next activity as they finish.

RECOGNITION OF SUCCESS

Keeping a record for each student showing tasks completed and effort made can help him or her to feel more valued as an individual in our class. Our mark book is for the student as well as for us. Simply by recording a quick impression mark, ticking to show that work is completed and letting students see their 'scores', we are demonstrating our interest in individual progress. The more we can demonstrate what someone **has** achieved, rather than **not** achieved, the more self esteem and confidence that person should gain and hence motivation to learn more (see *Boys' performance in Modern Foreign Languages,* p18, 4.1.3 'It helps if you know you are good … you have more confidence' and p31, 5.2).

It is common practice to mark written and spoken work using the National Curriculum criteria for the Attainment Targets and Levels. Looking at Table 2, p20, a student could get full marks for a Level 1 performance and be encouraged and helped to move up the Levels. This is a positive approach, allowing a person to climb his or her own ladder and not be left at the bottom of other people's. But what about activities where there is a final score? A vocabulary test, for example, or a 'Listen and note down' activity? To make this a positive experience for everyone, we could break the score down into three zones giving each one a colour. For example for a working total of 20:

<4–10>	<11–15>	<16–20>
Green (basic)	**Blue (middle)**	**Red (advanced)**

The score entered in the mark book is highlighted with the relevant colour. For example, a score of 5 would be highlighted green. Students could target either green, blue or red each time they do a task with a score. Someone who scores well in the green zone could be encouraged to try the blue. It is quick to see (for both teacher and student) when reading across the page of marks what has been achieved and the progress being made (see also *Boys' performance in Modern Foreign Languages,* p20, 4.4.1 'The teacher's focus and concern about their progress, however, was a key factor to their motivation').

The ideas and activities in the following chapters include some, or sometimes all of the seven ingredients above and have all been tried and tested in the classroom. Some may need adapting to suit your class, others you might want to avoid! Even then, however motivating we considered the activity to be, however lively, convinced and enthusiastic **we** are, the class is on occasions just not bothered. We choose the activity, therefore, according to the mood of our class, the day and the time.

Creating contexts, roles and links for activities within GCSE topic areas

Here we focus mainly on creating contexts and roles that mirror real-life events and situations that should catch the attention and imagination of our students. If we can link activities and projects to people and places, this can add a genuine purpose to the students' learning.

Adopting an adult, vocational dimension can take the students out of the classroom situation (see also *Something to say?,* Chapter 3, p60, 'Pupils' perceptions of Modern Languages in the curriculum). The board meeting simulation with Year 10 (see p13) gives us an example. We had a 'one voice rule', as one would in a board meeting, with a student as chairman and the teacher taking the minutes. The tables were arranged conference style. The students even removed their anoraks for this occasion. They had thought themselves out of the classroom and into an adult world situation and behaved accordingly.

We could also bring people in to talk with the students or arrange visits to places of work. Projects could then arise from these visits and be presented to the 'link' people. Year 10 made French adverts for the hotel with which they were linked and these were displayed in the hotel foyer. People taking them at face value as fellow adults had a wonderful effect not only on their self-esteem but also on their personal social skills and motivation. They wanted, and had the chance, to make a good impression. Other kinds of links can also engender positive personal and social interaction. Here are a few examples:

Doing things for:

- other classes   comic strip stories, booklets, flashcards, OHP acetates, etc;
- the rest of the class   writing a description of someone for the others to work out, making wordsearches and other games using computer software such as Puzzlemaker, a presentation using PowerPoint, or overhead transparencies (Discovery Schools at **www.puzzlemaker.com** provides a wealth of activities students can make, including wordsearches). See Chapter 8, where similar activities are put forward as extension work for early finishers.

In this chapter is a table of suggestions for contexts, links, roles and tasks, placed against a selection of GCSE topics. These ideas are based on teachers' suggestions in various INSET sessions over the last few years. They are a random collection of ideas and therefore do not always read across the columns. This table is followed by suggestions for activities related to three vocational topics.

	Contexts	Links	Roles	Tasks
Health and healthy living	• Seeing the school nurse • Football pitch • In the medical room • Dieting • At the chemist's here or abroad • In the doctor's surgery/ waiting room • Home and school	• The school nurse • A physio-therapist • A doctor • A chemist • Packaging for medicines and health products here and abroad	• Brain surgeon • Physio-therapist for footballers • Footballer • Interpreter in medical room for exchange guest • Exchange guest • Coroner • Hypo-chondriac • Counsellor for healthy living • Parent • Teacher	• Interview people in the links column – find out about their jobs, common problems, social skills, language needed, etc • Write sick notes for school • Read note from parents and give advice • Treat a footballer and give advice • Write instructions for taking medicine • Make a leaflet on healthy living • Make a phrase book for visiting the doctor's for the twin town, exchange school or pupils from own school going abroad
Travel and transport	• Transport of local goods to places abroad	• The transport and delivery section of a local department store or supermarket	• Interviewer • Publisher of support service for drivers travelling abroad	• Interview a driver who goes abroad to discover any problems he or she faces • Prepare a cultural guide for abroad, e.g. how to get served in a French café • Prepare a linguistic guide containing such sections as language needed for breakdowns, accommodation, service station, etc

Contexts	Links	Roles	Tasks
Holiday activities	• The school trip • The exchange visit	• Other teachers and pupils to find out language needs • The town twinning committee	• Publisher • Writer • Editor • Researcher – to research language needs	• Make brochures and leaflets • Prepare and give a PowerPoint presentation • Make a cassette recording of attractions and activities • Interpret a brochure giving local attractions • Make a phrase book for pupils in Years 7 and 8 going on the school trip or exchange • Make a phrase book for the exchange visitors in school and in the town
Weather	• Television • Radio • Internet	• Local television or radio broadcaster or interviewer • Newspaper weather correspon-dent • School or local website master • Internet	• Television or radio announcer • Person responsible for updating weather pages for website • Researcher • Newspaper correspon-dent • Listener on radio weather phone-in programme • Telephone operator on phone-in weather programme and callers	• Prepare and present the weather forecast on radio, television, Web page – either for peers to watch or for international tourists • Phone-in simulation for latest weather report • Television or radio presenter rings locals spread around the county to ask them what the weather is like and make some general small talk (this happens in Cumbria)

IDEAS FOR WRITTEN PROJECT WORK WITH A VOCATIONAL SLANT

The essential nature of all these activities is that they are open-ended. This means that the the students, although they have a core language as a basis, can decide on the content and format and be creative. Ideas for these activities are listed under individual projects and group projects by topic. Furthermore, group projects lend themselves well to differentiation, including all students in the end result. A group of four to five students could take a particular area of a topic and each contribute a section of it. Under the guidance of the teacher individuals could choose to do something appropriate for their level of performance. For example, in the bar and restaurant topic below, one student might label pictures of dishes offered in the style of the 'Little Chef' menus (AT4 Levels 1–2), another might attempt descriptions of these dishes. This could stretch from AT4 Levels 3–5 or even more, depending on the complexity of the language.

Working in a bar or restaurant

Students work individually
1 Design and label a poster for a hotel or conference centre for the foreign customer, showing the types of activities and other facilities that are available.
2 Draw a map of the hotel or conference centre and label the rooms and facilities.
3 Design a menu for foreign customers.
4 Make signs in the foreign language for the hotel or conference centre.

Students work in groups

Design and prepare a brochure or information pack for the hotel or conference centre or even the local MacDonald's, including:

1 opening hours;

2 facilities offered with times and days;

3 a labelled plan of the hotel or conference centre;

4 leisure activities which are possible, e.g. darts, dominoes;

5 descriptions of drinks;

6 descriptions of dishes on the menu;

7 a price list for drinks in the foreign language;

8 a detailed menu, with descriptions of dishes and prices;

9 a list of useful phrases for foreign clients;

10 a list of useful phrases for the waiter, waitress, or people who work behind the bar.

Working in the Leisure industry

Students work individually	Students work in groups
1 Design and label a poster for a town or leisure centre for the foreign visitor, showing the types of leisure activities that are available.	'What's on in town?' could be a pack containing information on: **1** activities – times/days/dates/duration; **2** the groups of people they are suitable for; **3** prices, methods of payment and special concessions; **4** a plan of the local leisure centre.
2 Draw a map of a leisure centre or town and label the places on it.	
3 Design a booking-in form for foreign visitors which could be used in a leisure centre.	'Leisure centre activities' could be a pack including information on: **1** activities – times/days/dates/location; **2** groups of people; **3** prices, methods of payment, special concessions; **4** hiring equipment.
4 Categorise films which can be seen under film types and illustrate.	

Working in accommodation reception – Hotels and Campsites

Students work individually	Students work in groups **A** and **B**
1 Design and label a poster for a hotel or campsite for the foreign visitor, showing the types of leisure activities and other facilities that are available.	**A** Topic – A hotel brochure showing: **1** rooms available; **2** when the hotel is open; **3** special bargains; **4** facilities offered; **5** leisure activities which are possible, e.g. fishing, golf; **6** methods of payment.
2 Draw a map of a hotel or campsite and label the rooms and facilities.	
3 Design a booking-in form for foreign visitors.	**B** Topic – Information pack on campsites in the area showing: **1** details and number of pitches and prices; **2** opening times; **3** location of the campsites; **4** facilities; **5** activities; **6** methods of payment; **7** hiring equipment.
4 Make signs in the foreign language for a local hotel or campsite.	

MAKING ACTIVITIES FOR OTHERS TO USE

The following activities are adaptable to any topic. They are not aimed at the place of work, but are practice activities which the students can prepare for their peers to use. Although the end results are practice activities for their peers, the production of them is open-ended, because the author chooses which language to use and how to present it. This is why these are suggested as good extension activities in Chapter 8.

1 Make cards for language games, for example, dominoes, matching, or teach and test. For teach and test, the students could each make eight cards, drawing on one side of each card and writing the matching word on the reverse side. They could then test a partner and then other members of the class (see p38).

2 Create a board game drawing on the vocabulary for names of sports, rooms in a leisure centre, drinks and food available in the bar, etc (see p49).

5 Activities for presenting new language and topics

In Chapter 4 we focused on the importance of establishing contexts, roles and links wherever possible in order for the students to be able to relate what they are learning to their own lives. In this and subsequent chapters are suggestions for activities for presentation, repetition and practice of new or recycled language. In Chapter 9, we look at how we can fit these into a lesson or series of lessons, taking the students through a logical and natural progression of the theme and the language connected to it. Elements of these activities might be familiar to you, for they are not claiming to be original. The emphasis is on adapting them to allow maximum involvement and participation. We do this in four main ways:

1 Getting students doing things.
2 Making sure they see the point of doing things.
3 Ensuring they can all be included in the activity by differentiating where necessary.
4 Allowing for personal interest and social interaction student-to-student, student-to-teacher and even to other teachers in the school.

You might like to map these activities against the seven ingredients for motivation (see p17).

PRESENTING LANGUAGE

We outline four activities for presenting new language or revising:

1 Students generate language (see also Part 2: *Yes – but will they behave?*, p77, 'Listing').
2 Students share personal information.
3 Students link characters to well-known people.
4 Students take notes as the teacher presents a story line.

Students generate language

Getting the class to generate language is a popular way to begin a topic. In the activity below we attempt to iron out the pitfalls that can arise and to ensure full involvement. For example, there is the risk that they (or we) won't know the words in the foreign language, that, if in groups, they'll leave all the work to one person and just chat or that when we feed back they won't listen to the people suggesting ideas.

As a presentation activity for the topic: 'What to do and see around the town', students – in groups of four or five – generate language for all the places a foreign tourist might like to go in their town (see right).

Procedure	**Rationale and notes**
1 As students come up with ideas they each write them down on their personal copy – see Student's sheet below. They can write either in English or the FL – or use dictionaries.	Keep them all busy. **Get everyone to write down the ideas the group thinks up** – keep them all involved. Recognise effort. **Take their sheets in later to check their effort** (note it in the mark book) – shows we are interested in their individual effort.
2 Have the words we have planned to teach covered on the OHT, or ready to display on the smart board. As students give us ideas, we give points to the ones who get words we have listed. Add new ideas on a different part of the board.	**This means we are able to teach what we have planned,** while making the class feel they have thought of the same thing plus extra ideas.
3 The students tick their list as they hear the words they had also thought of and add the new ones.	**Students can see what they have and what is left** It keeps them busy! **They build up a repertoire of language for a later activity,** which might be creating a poster or leaflet.
4 **Variation on 3, if the students do not copy down the extra language:** After the lesson, working from the students' sheets, we can produce a chart or OHT version of the extra language chosen by the students for use later on.	**We may want an accurate version.** It also allows for time to double check the FL for English words they give us that were difficult to translate on the spur of the moment. **Personal involvement.** The OHT of language from the students could be revealed word for word, students look at their lists and claim it if it was theirs.

Student's sheet

Was kann man in Carlisle machen?

Gruppe ____ Name ____

Punkte ____

Ideen:

Teacher's OHT

Mann kann	ins Café ins Kino	gehen.
	die Stadt das Schloß	besuchen.
	Tennis Golf	spielen.
	im Restaurant im Gasthaus	essen.

Teaching or revising dates using the students' birthdays

Presenting the language for dates can be a bit dry! To capture interest, we could relate dates to the birthdays of the students. See below for an example of a card made by one of the students.

	Procedure	Rationale and notes
1	Before the lesson, place a piece of card and a felt-tip pen on each desk.	This gives the impression something is going to happen and also saves hassle with giving things out. Have a student responsible for checking in the pens.
2	When the students have settled (or as they enter the room), show a card you have made for yourself as an example. Ask them to write their name on one side of the card and their birthday **in figures** on the other.	Get them doing! **This technique gets the class doing something practical straight away.** The cards are useful for practice activities later on. Students are writing about themselves, it is manageable and creative, they all have the necessary materials, so are likely to settle down.
3	Put a list of their names on the OHT, Smartboard or whiteboard.	**Time management.** This can double up as the register check.
4	As they complete the cards, go through the list and ask each student, 'Wann hast du Geburtstag?' The student shows you his or her card. You say the date and copy it **in figures** on the OHT against his or her name (see table overleaf).	**Non-threatening.** The students are not confident to **say** the dates yet. This way **they hear the language in the background and become familiar with it.** **Personal interest.** The students are interested to know each other's birthdays – and to let others know about theirs.
5	As they complete their cards, get students to copy the list of birthdays in their books.	**Purpose.** Tell students they need the list in their books for a Lotto game later and also in order to be able to send each other birthday cards!

Example of a student's card

front

back

Classic Pathfinder 2: *Challenging classes*

The birthday list may look like this:

Name	Geburtstag	Name	Geburtstag
Frau Alison	2.3	Nicola	22.1
Katie	20.8	Julie	23.8
Darren	13.12	Andy	18.4

This technique could also be used in different contexts. For example, presenting likes and dislikes. The students draw a picture of what they like doing on the back of their cards, instead of their birthdays. It is a good way to present the topic of families, because it lets them give you the information they want to give about such a personal, sensitive and sometimes complicated matter.

PRESENTING CHARACTER TRAITS USING WELL-KNOWN PEOPLE

The aim here is to introduce words and structures for talking and writing about character.

	Procedure	Rationale and notes
1	Place a piece of card and a felt-tip pen on each desk before the class enters.	**Expectation.** This gives the impression something is going to happen **Organisation.** It saves hassle with giving things out. Have a student responsible for checking in the pens.
2	As students come in get them to write the name of a well-known person on the card in large attractive writing.	Keep them busy and allowing for latecomers. **If they are given something to do as they come in they are likely to settle down better and not be disturbed by latecomers.** This is **personal** – they can express their own interests.
3	As they finish students stick the cards with Blu-tack around the edge of the OHP screen – early finishers do another one!	**Purpose** for making the card attractive is that it will be displayed. **Personal involvement.** Sticking up their cards allows them to be personally involved. **Keep early finishers busy.**

<table>
<tr><td>④</td><td>Put a list of character traits on OHP (see below for French and German versions). Give the students a photocopy of it.</td></tr>
</table>

Leaving nothing to chance. Using a photocopy saves the problem of trying to get them to draw a grid in their books – and **ensures a reasonably well presented reference sheet.**

<table>
<tr><td>⑤</td><td>Reveal the sentences one by one. With each sentence: get the students to arrive at the meaning of the word by giving clues (paraphrase, mime, etc); write the English for the word against it on the right; get the students to suggest a person to fit the description; write in the name for them with the English for the adjective. Students then copy this down.</td></tr>
</table>

Physical engagement. This is the teacher-controlled part, which tends to invite disruption, so keep students busy by filling out the list at the same time as us.

Purpose – 'What are we doing that for?' Tell students they will need the list for their worksheet and for the posters they will make.

Support. We are writing in the English for them to copy, because many may have short memories. If they forget a word they can become very frustrated and give up – often leading to disruptive behaviour.

Personal choice – let the class take the lead. If they want to insert a name of their own – we let them. They will very quickly want to insert the names of their peers and of teachers in the school. This can lead to positive social interaction, if carefully engineered by us!

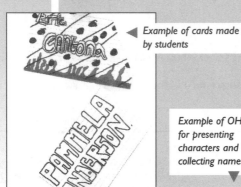

◀ *Example of cards made by students*

Example of OHTs for presenting characters and collecting names
▼

1	Ken Dodd	ist	lustig	fun
2	Frau Dodds	ist	nett	nice
3	Britney	ist	beliebt	popular
4	Herr Evans	ist	schüchtern	shy
5		ist	nervös	
6		ist	intellektuel	
7		ist	ruhig	
8		ist	dumm	
9		ist	faul	
10		ist	attraktiv	

This activity is far more straightforward in German as we do not have to think about adjective agreements after ist.

	1	Harry Potter	est	timide	shy
	2	Chris Tarrant	est	calme	calm
	3	Tom Cruise	est	cool	cool
	4		est	gentil	
	5		est	intelligent	
	1	Kylie	est	timide	shy
	2	Mme Jones	est	calme	calm
	3	Pamela	est	cool	cool
	4		est	gentil**le**	
	5		est	intelligent**e**	

Classic Pathfinder 2: *Challenging classes*

Taking notes

Here the teacher is presenting the new language of daily routine embedded in a personal story, accompanied by pictures if possible.

	Procedure	Rationale and notes
1	Students to have paper and pens ready.	**Expectation.** This gives the impression something is going to happen – they are going to be doing something.
2	Tell them you are about to tell a story and they are to jot down anything they understand – do a trial run with the first sentence or two.	**Personal involvement.** It is usually more successful if the story is about the teacher or someone in the class, as this makes it more personal. **Encouragement.** It is important to emphasise they jot down everything they understand – that it all counts for the final feedback – they may hear something others didn't.
3	Tell the story – allowing students to note down what they can.	**Get them doing.** We cannot expect challenging classes to just sit and listen – doing something like this gives them an active reason for paying attention.
4	Feed back by inviting people to tell you in the FL or in English what they have understood.	**Confidence.** They should be confident and enthusiastic to tell you what they have understood because they have their jottings to help them and like to have spotted things others didn't.
5	Students tick their sheets as they hear the points mentioned and add anything extra they heard. They get a point for every detail.	**Differentiation.** This allows all students to perform at their own level. Some students will have noted 'main points and some details' (AT1 Level 4) and even understood parts where you used tenses, for example 'Last week I got up at six every morning ... next week it will be different' (AT1 Level 5). Some may only catch some main points and opinions (AT1 Level 3).
6	They write down their final score and the teacher collects it into the mark book later.	**Recognition of success.** You could follow the suggestion on p23, for example 3–6 facts, Green; 7–10, Blue; 11 or more, Red. This means everyone can feel successful at his or her own level.

6 Activities for language recognition

Having presented a topic, we need to get students to recognise the associated structures and words when they hear them. They are more likely to listen carefully if we can make sure they have an active purpose for doing so. In each of the activities below they have to listen and **do** something, i.e. give a physical response, a short verbal response or note something down. In order to demonstrate how we can continue in the context we have set, each activity has a dialogue relevant to it. We are assuming in all of them that the class has learnt to ask the question. The activities are transferable to most topics.

CHAOTIC LISTENING

Preparation

- Write a short story including new words in a topic, making sure that the key words feature frequently (see French and German examples on the right).
- Prepare flashcards or magazine pictures representing each key word.

Activity

- Divide the class into as many groups as there are flashcards and give each group a flashcard.
- Tell the students they must jump up and sit down again quickly whenever they hear the key word for which they have the flashcard.
- As you read out the story, groups leap up and down as they hear their word. It is also fun to have a word where they must **all** leap up. In the French example on the right, this word is *passe-temps* (the German version doesn't have one).

Les passe-temps

You need flashcards for: le shopping, la voile, le rugby, le squash, le football, la pêche

Bon, alors, il y en a beaucoup! Si vous me demandez quels sont mes **passe-temps** préférés, eh bien, c'est le **shopping**! Comme je ne suis pas très bien organisée, le **shopping**, je le fais n'importe quand. Mais la plupart font leur **shopping** le vendredi ou le samedi.

Un de mes autres **passe-temps**, en famille cette fois, c'est la **voile** – oui, on fait de la **voile** plutôt pendant les vacances. Mon mari, lui, fait du **rugby**. Le samedi il s'entraîne et le dimanche il joue au **rugby**. Vous aimez regarder le **rugby** à la télé? Moi, non, je préfère le **shopping**. Mon mari m'accompagne pour faire le **shopping** mais uniquement dans les magasins de sports. Vous savez – ces magasins specialisés où l'on trouve tout pour le sport, depuis la raquette de tennis, de ping-pong, de **squash**, jusqu'au matériel pour la **pêche** en passant par les ballons de **rugby,** etc.

Mon fils ne joue pas au **rugby** – il préfère le **football**. Alors, vous imaginez le samedi après-midi devant la télé où se succèdent les matchs de **football**, de **rugby**; le **squash** c'est plus rare.

Quant à la **pêche** – n'en parlons pas! Cette année pendant les vacances nous essaierons aussi d'aller à la **pêche** – vous savez, la **pêche** à la traîne que l'on peut faire à bord d'un bateau?

Et si je vous demande quels sont vos **passe-temps,** vous me répondez quoi? La **pêche**? Le **rugby**? Le **shopping**? Le **football**? Le cinéma? La drague? La **voile**? Les boules?

On a le choix, non? En tout cas moi, mon **passe-temps** c'est pas de vous parler des **passe-temps**. Salut!

Die Freizeit

You need flashcards for: Fußball, Golf, reiten, tanzen, kegeln, angeln, segeln, einkaufen.

Na ja! Wenn man **Fußball** gern hat, kann man **Fußball** jeden Tag anschauen. **Golf** zu spielen ist ziemlich teuer und **reiten** gehen noch teurer.

Reiten und **Golf** mache ich nicht gern und **kegeln gehen** ist langweilig! Ganz oft gehe ich **tanzen**. Hier in der Stadt kann man jeden abend **tanzen** und **kegeln** gehen. Ich weiß aber nicht, wo man **Golf** spielen kann.

Wenn man aufs Land fährt, kann man **angeln** und **reiten** gehen. Es ist auch möglich **Fußball** und **Golf** zu spielen. Ob man auf dem Land **kegeln** gehen kann, weiß ich nicht! Man kann auf dem See **segeln** gehen – man sagt, das ist sehr schön!

Ich mag aber nicht **segeln**. **Einkaufen** mag ich! Während meine Freunde **Fußball** oder **Golf** spielen, **reiten** oder **kegeln** gehen, gehe ich **einkaufen**! Ich muß neue Schuhe **kaufen**, denn ich gehe heute abend **tanzen**. Mein Freund braucht einen neuen Hut fürs **Golf** Spielen. Ich muß auch Drinks für eine Party **kaufen**.

Hier kann man schließlich viel machen. **Fußball** und **Golf** spielen, **reiten** gehen, **tanzen** gehen, **kegeln** oder **segeln** gehen, **einkaufen** gehen. Meine Stadt ist wunderbar!

BEAT THE TEACHER

Preparation

- Prepare flashcards or magazine pictures representing new language for the topic. For example, drinks.
- Have a score table on the board, a column for you and one for the class.

Activity

- Hold the flashcards (see below) in batches of four to five, with the pictures facing the class.
- Don't look at the pictures, and make a show of trying to remember each one as you hold it by saying, *'Je voudrais un thé'* (*'Ich möchte einen Tee'*), etc.
- Tell the class to shout in the FL: if it is correct, *'Oui, voilà'* (*'Ja, kommt gleich'*); or if it is not correct, *'Je regrette, il n'y en a pas'* (*'Leider gibt's nicht'*).
- Mark up points.
- Make an act of 'getting in a state' each time you are wrong and being relieved when you are right! This technique can be used with any topic and set of flashcards.

front of card

| un jus de cassis | un jus d'orange | un jus de pomme | un chocolat chaud | un thé | un café |

back of card

GRAB A CARD!

This game is adaptable to any context, but for this demonstration we will use a dialogue, as above, for ordering drinks.

Preparation

- Two sets of flashcards (see above) with the pictures facing upwards around the room on the desks.
- Write numbers you give students in a row on the board (as reminder for you).
- Make two columns for team points below.

Activity

- Divide the class into two teams and number the students in each team, e.g.1–15.

- Call a number and tick it on your list, e.g. *'Numéro trois!'*.
- The two students with that number race to stand.
- Do this once more with a different number.
- Next time do the same then get the class to ask, *'Vous désirez?'*
- Respond with *'Je voudrais + ...'* giving the FL for one of the pictures.
- The first to dash and grab the picture and say *'Voilà'* wins a point for his or her team.

Getting the teams to help the two people racing to find the card encourages collaboration and saves less-confident students being embarrassed by failure. Note that the students must replace the pictures each time.

 ## TELEPATHY

This can only be done once per class, but it captures the students totally.

Preparation

- Prepare a chart or OHT of a grid containing numbers of hotel rooms.
- Before the lesson, seek out a few members of the class and entrust them with your secret, which is, if you point to the bottom right hand corner, they say *'Non'* (*'Nein'*) if you point to the middle of the number, they say *'Oui'* (*'Ja'*).

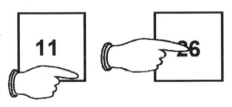

Activity

- Display the OHT of hotel room numbers.
- Send one of the students, who knows your secret, out of the room.
- Get the class to choose a number.
- The student comes back in and looks at the OHT while you call out the numbers saying each time, *'Chambre numéro + number?'*
- If you point to the middle, the student says, *'Non'*.
- If you point to bottom corner, the student says, *'Oui, c'est ça'*.

While absorbed by trying to work out how the student knew which number had been chosen, the class hear the FL for the numbers over and over again.

This is a chance to allow students who do not shine linguistically to play an important and enviable part in the lesson. For a variation on this, play the game using flashcards, the sign being the way you hold the card.

MINI-TESTS

Preparation

- The topic here is taking a bar snack order from a foreign visitor.
- Put an OHT of numbered pictures of foods on the OHP (see below).

Activity

- Elicit from the class the question *'Vous désirez?'*
- Choose a picture, note down the number and say, *'Je prends du poulet'*.
- Students choose the picture that represents 'chicken' and write the number down.
- Do two more.
- Feed back to the class.
- Get a show of hands for three correct, count the hands and write the number on the board.
- Do another mini-test to see if the class can better its score.

We can support students in several ways. Some students might be disadvantaged, because they have trouble transferring information from the board/screen into their books. They might choose to use a photocopy of the OHT, a help sheet, so they can place it on their table nearer where they are writing. We might also differentiate the content of the test by including a cognate or easy word with each mini-test to ensure everyone gets at least one out of the three. As extension, a student confident with the pronunciation might like to be the teacher. A variation of this is to play it as a team game, counting the hands raised for each team and noting them on the board.

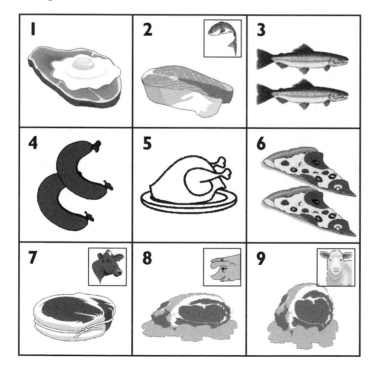

KEY

Je prends du/de la/ des/de l'...

1 œuf-jambon
2 saumon
3 truite
4 saucisses
5 poulet
6 pizza
7 rôti de bœuf
8 rôti de porc
9 rôti d'agneau

7 Activities for pronouncing and remembering language

As we move into activities to help students pronounce and remember the language, we often come up against problems. This is because we are using ourselves as the spoken model, so this part of the lesson is often teacher centred. With some classes, the activities below may not yet be possible or we will probably wait for the day when they are at their best. These activities have been used successfully with lower sets in Years 9 and 10, mainly because they have two important ingredients in common: students are repeating language in chorus, which means they do not stand out; and the activities appeal to the different senses, being either visual, auditory, kinaesthetic or all three at once.

 ## CHANTS AND RHYTHMS

Together with the students we find a rhythm or chant or pop song into which they can fit the language. If we can get this going it is a good way of helping them lose their inhibitions, because their individual effort is lost in the noise of the chorus. Sometimes it takes the form of us entertaining the class (is she off her head?) but it does sink in – even if they are not joining in at the right time. The example below illustrates repetition of the vocabulary for clothing to ''Ere we go' the undying, very repetitive football chant. This has a high success rate and will accommodate any language.

Preparation

Actual clothes are best, magazine pictures of clothes next best – otherwise flashcards.

Activity

- Hold up, for example, a shirt.

- Get students to chant with you *Une chemise, une chemise, une chemise, une chemise, une chemise, une chemise,* etc.

- Continue chanting and pick up, for example, the tie. *Une cravate, une cravate, une cravate, une cravate, une cravate, une cravate,* etc.

- Get volunteers out to orchestrate the chant, holding up different pieces of clothing at random. The song could now sound like this, depending on the flashcard held up.

Une chemise, une cravate, un manteau,
un manteau, une chaussette, une cravate, etc.

Almost anything can be fitted into this tune. For example, the perfect tense:

J'ai mangé, j'ai dormi, j'ai acheté, etc.

As extension, this could be the basis for students to make up their own songs as an open-ended activity later.

RHYTHM

Year 10 in Chapter 1 took a long time to master the question, *'Je peux vous aider?'*. Find a particularly catchy chant for the phrase or question and clap as you repeat it to the rhythm and try to get them to join in. If they do not, it is still useful, because when you want to elicit the question from them you can clap or tap the rhythm as a reminder. ('It's a good idea that rhythm effort, it helps you remember it' – praise indeed from Year 10!)

SIT DOWN IF YOU SAY IT

This activity is good for emphasising single words that are particularly difficult to pronounce.

Preparation

Write up the sentence to be repeated. The example here is the German, *'Kann ich Ihnen helfen?'* (Can I help you?). The targeted word here is *Ihnen,* so we underline it.

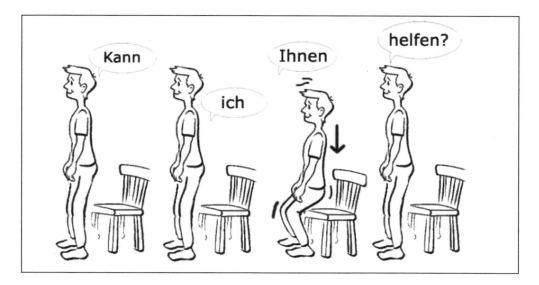

Activity

- Get the whole class to stand.
- Go round the students clockwise in turn, getting them each to say one word of the sentence.
- The students who have to say *Ihnen* must sit down.
- Keep going round and round the class, keeping to the same order, until only one person is left.
- That person is the winner.

HASSLE LINES

Preparation

A magazine picture of a smiling person and another one of a miserable person. Stick them on the whiteboard with speech bubbles.

Smiling person   *J'aime faire ça! (Das mache ich gern)*
Miserable person   *Je n'aime pas faire ça! (Das mache ich nicht gern)*

Activity

- Point to the smiling face symbol and get the class to repeat a few times, *'J'aime faire ça!'* Do this dramatically!
- Do the same with the miserable face, getting the class to repeat, *'Je n'aime pas faire ça!'*
- Divide the class into two halves, one half negative and the other positive. Get them to argue against each other, each side repeating their phrase with more and more feeling.
- Get them to do this in pairs and choose the most dramatic pair to demonstrate to the class.

You can do this with any positive and negative statements, for example, *'Je (ne) veux (pas) aller en ville'* (*'Ich will (nicht) in die Stadt fahren!'*).

For differentiation, encourage students to add any other language they know, such as opinions.

This activity allows the good actors to shine as well as it being a repetition activity.

FORWARD AND BACKWARD CHAINING

This is effective for helping students to pronounce and remember long words or phrases.

Preparation

- Split words into single syllables, or split sentences and phrases into single words.

Activity

Build up the word or phrase (forwards then backwards) with the class in chorus. Here are two examples:

- Building up the French word for 'Tourist Office': *syn ... syndi ... syndicat ... syndicat d'i ... syndicat d'ini ... syndicat d'initia ... syndicat d'initiative!*
- The German word for 'bus stop': *le ... stelle ... testelle ... haltestelle ... Bushaltestelle.*

MIMES FOR THE ALPHABET

Active use of the alphabet is necessary for giving and receiving information, for example, if booking someone in over the phone. One way of helping the students to remember how the letters of the alphabet are pronounced is to make up mimes for each letter. Here are a few examples of mimes used with Year 10 of the French alphabet. Four mimes were thought up by the teacher, and the rest by the students.

Open mouth, put finger in, say '**Ahh**' as though for the doctor

Swimming movement (in the **bay**)

Make a speaking gesture with hand – **say**

Opening curtains, to greet the **day**

Point to a mess on the floor and say, '**Eugh**!'

Flick (imaginary!) cigarette. Crash the **ash**

Drive **car**

Point down to '**ell**

Play snooker – with **cue**

Hold your **(h)air**

Drink **thé**

As a variation, numbers can be treated in the same way.

Students who cannot shine linguistically may well have very good ideas for mimes and can have a valuable part to play here and feel involved.

FASTER THAN THE TEACHER

Preparation

- An OHT showing foods or activities, for example. A stop-watch.

Activity

- Teacher reads through the list of activities and the students time him or her.
- Students then do this in groups, to find the fastest in each group.
- Group winners compete with one another.
- The overall winner competes with the teacher.

Allowing students to practise in groups before individuals compete with the teacher ensures that everyone has a go.

8   Activities for practising language

The activities chosen here can all be carried out independently. We will first look at Listening and Speaking activities and then at those which involve Reading and Writing. We have chosen here simple straightforward activities that allow for several variations. Their simplicity makes them ideal as routines for practising language. What we are aiming for is to create a safe environment in which the students have clear routines as a scaffold. Routines also save us having to give complicated instructions, which is especially difficult with classes who do not allow us to finish a sentence!

ACTIVITIES FOCUSING ON LISTENING AND SPEAKING

Listening and Speaking activities are often more difficult to run than Reading and Writing, especially in classes where students are easily distracted. It helps to be conscious of three factors: **support, purpose** and **management**.

Support

Lack of support can lead to insecurity in a task and then to withdrawal or even disruption. If an activity is unsuccessful, rather than abandon the idea in the future, it might be useful to reflect upon the following points:

1   Was there a clear, simple **structure**?

2   Were the **instructions** clear and available for reference, in case students forgot, or didn't understand what we said? For example, in addition to our instructions, the rules of a game could be written on the board or OHT.

3   Did the activity rely heavily on **memory**? Did the students have access to an *aide-mémoire* either on the wall, in a glossary or in their files?

4   Were there opportunities for differentiation, so all students could be included?

Purpose, challenge and incentive

Students respond well to challenges to remember and to think (see also *Reflections on motivation* 'ICT makes it click', p80, where Jim McElwee found that, 'physically moving the text helped the pupils understand the grammatical context'). The activities here focus on teaching and testing in pairs or groups, because, in addition to the challenge to think, the one being tested can measure his or her success and the one testing feels powerful having all the answers! All the activities have these important features in common:

- One person has the answers in order to check responses.
- There is a tangible result, for example a score is kept.
- There is a tactile element, so students feel they are doing something.

Management

We can avoid complicated instructions and confusion by running an activity first with the whole class and then moving them into groups or pairs. Once the activity becomes a routine, we can leave out the whole class run-through if appropriate.

CARDS	The following activities are suggestions for teaching and testing Listening and Speaking using cards and a board game.

 ## WIN THE CARD

Preparation

- Make sets of cards for each group with the picture on the front and the FL on the back (see p38).
- Divide the class into groups of three or four.

Activity

- The group leader holds the set of cards, with the pictures facing outwards and reveals the pictures one by one.
- Anyone knowing the response needed knocks on the desk and gives the FL.
- The group leader checks this against the back of the card and gives it to him or her if correct. If not, he or she continues to hold it there until someone gets it right.
- The winner is the one with the most cards, when they have all been used up.
- The winner gets a point.
- The students take it in turns to be the leader.

Example dialogue: Leader   *Vous désirez comme boisson?*
                   Contestants   *Je voudrais* + item.
                   Leader   *Voilà* (if correct)/*Il n'y en a pas* (if incorrect).

As a variation, the students could keep a score of how many cards they win each time then add them up at the end to see who got the most – in the group and also in the class.

Taking it in turns to be the leader rather than the winner doing this, ensures that even the less confident students can have a powerful moment!

TEACH AND TEST IN PAIRS

Preparation

- Make sets of cards with the picture on the front and the FL on the back.
- Divide the class into pairs.

Activity

A tests **B,** putting the cards **B** is not sure of aside and retesting until **B** can get them all right.

DIFFERENTIATED TEACH AND TEST CARDS

The cards could contain sentences or words with gaps on the front and the missing words on the back. This way the cards work both ways! See the example below.

Preparation

- Assuming you want the students to practise the language in a dialogue, divide this up into separate sentences and phrases.
- On each card, write the phrase on side A with one or two gaps with the same phrase but different gaps on side B. The phrase is *Je peux vous aider? (Kann ich Ihnen helfen?),* thus:

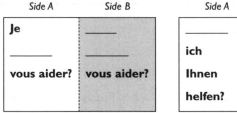

Side A	Side B		Side A	Side B
Je	_____		_____	Kann
_____	_____		ich	_____
vous aider?	vous aider?		Ihnen	_____
			helfen?	helfen?

- You can see that side B is more challenging.
- The examples below have been prepared in Word, and need to be cut up and side B folded onto the back of side A and stuck.

Activity

This activity is played in the same way as the 'Teach and test in pairs' above. Get students to play with side **A** facing first and then, when confident, to attempt the activity with side **B** facing.

Early finishers can make cards for others to do.

Side A	Side B
Bonj____ **Madame!**	**____jour** **____!**

Side A	Side B
Je ne **_____** **pas** **anglais.**	**____ ____** **parle** **_____** **anglais.**

Side A	Side B
Pas de **_____!**	**____ ____** **problème!**

Side A	Side B
Je parle **un peu** **_____.**	**____ _____** **____ ____** **français.**

Side A	Side B
Mais **c'est** **_____!**	**_____** **_____** **formidable!**

Side A	Side B
Je **_____** **vous aider?**	**____** **peux** **____ ____?**

 ## TEACH AND TEST AS A BOARD GAME

Preparation

- To make the gameboard, divide a card into numbered squares, each with a picture of the relevant topic language (see example below).
- Supply a die and counters for each group. (The students can make their counters from a small piece of card, on which they write their initial.)
- Make a checklist with all the answers against the numbers that appear on the board (see example below).
- Organise the class into pairs or small groups. They then choose a team leader who has the checklist.

Activity

- Each student throws the die to see who gets the highest score. That person starts.
- They then take it in turns to throw the die.
- They move their counter along the board according to the number on their die.
- They must say the FL for the picture in the square they land on.
- The team leader checks it against the checklist.
- If the answer is acceptable the player stays there.
- If the leader or group need to help the contestant then he or she moves one square back.
- The first player to reach the end is the winner.
- NB each player has only one go at a time.

Moving back just one square rather than to where they were before throwing the die, means that students who have difficulties with the language still have a chance to win. However, even if helped by the others, a student **must** make an attempt at the language to be able to move his or her counter at all.

Checklist for the leader	6	une bibliothèque	12	maçon
1 infirmière	7	un bar	13	en chômage
2 agent de police	8	militaire	14	en retraite
3 professeur	9	le coiffeur	15	mécanicien
4 une station service	10	un collège		
5 un bureau	11	un restaurant		

PEN & PAPER	The following activities are suggestions for teaching and testing Listening and Speaking using paper and pen.

GIVE US A CLUE – SMALL GROUPS

Here students guess a hidden date, time or price following clues given by the leader.

Preparation

- Get the class into small groups. They then elect a leader.
- The leader needs paper and a pen.

Activity

We will use **time** here as an example.

- The leader writes a time on his or her paper, hides it, then asks *'C'est à quelle heure?'* (*'Wann passiert das?'*)
- The others guess the time and are guided in by the leader saying *'C'est trop tard/tôt'* (*'Das ist zu spät/früh),* until someone gets it right.
- The one who gets it right becomes the leader.

The winning of this game is in the guessing. Students could choose whether they use their books to help them with the language.

TEACH AND TEST USING EACH OTHER'S BOOKS OR FILES – IN PAIRS

Preparation

This activity can take place once the students have the language in their books, perhaps copied out after an exercise such as mix and match or simply vocabulary written out.

Activity (with vocabulary books)

- **A** and **B** swap books.
- **A** tests **B** on what is there and ticks the words **B** gets right, then signs against the score at the bottom. They then swap. They could do this until they get all the words right.

Activity (with a matching-up exercise – pictures and words or phrases)

- **A** keeps his or her book for reference, but hides the contents from **B**.
- **A** takes **B**'s book and covers the words.
- As **B** remembers the words correctly, **A** ticks them and adds a score and signature at the bottom.
- They then swap over.

Students who have extreme difficulties writing accurately might choose to use a photocopy of the language to ensure they can take part in this activity.

To differentiate, the score could be in Green, Blue, Red zones (see p23).

Adding spice to 'teach and test'

Preparation

As above, but the students also need to draw a noughts and crosses grid.

Activity

The same procedure as above is used for testing each other, except that, rather than go through the whole sheet and then swap, students alternate after each go.

- **A** chooses crosses and **B** noughts.
- When **A** is testing **B,** if **B** gets one wrong, **A** can place a cross on the grid. If **B** gets it right, **B** places a nought on the grid.
- Then **B** tests **A** and so on. *(Thanks to Anna Downey, for this)*

ACTIVITIES FOCUSING ON READING AND WRITING

Reading and Writing activities are often easier to run than Listening and Speaking. It still helps, however, to be conscious of the same three classroom management factors: **support, purpose** and **management**.

Support

Is there enough support? Do the students know where to find help? Is there an adapted version of the task for students who have difficulty?

Purpose

We can make Reading and Writing practice more relevant to the students by, for example, imitating activities in popular magazines.

Management

Keep instructions simple. In the following activities, students will be working either individually, collaboratively with their partner or in groups.

DECIPHERING A CODE IN FIGURES

Students may find it helpful to work in pairs or small groups. Working in this way is less threatening and encourages students to collaborate, using each other's strengths. Before they begin, it would be a good idea point out strategies they could use, by doing some with them. For example, having found the letter for one item of code, they could search the text for similar ones, rather than plough through one figure after the next.

Preparation

- The alphabet is represented by numbers.
- On the conversion table, the numbers are written in words. For complete accuracy, you might decide to give accented letters their own number, for example, *é* or *è* in French, *ä*, or *ö* in German and in Spanish *ú* or *ñ*. This could bring your alphabet to, say, 36 letters. You put them all in a table (as letters **a** and **b** below) and attribute the numbers 1–36 to these letters at random, with the numbers written in words alongside, e.g. *seize* and *vingt-deux*.

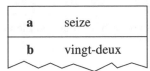

| **a** | seize |
| **b** | vingt-deux |

- Underline capital letters.
- You now write the text in figures instead of letters, e.g. *Bonjour!* might look like this:

<u>22</u>, 24, 11, 4, 24, 2, 9!

Activity

- The students look at the figures given in the message, e.g. <u>22</u>, find the word for it on the conversion sheet, e.g. vingt-deux, and write the corresponding letter, i.e. **B**, on the message.
- Early finishers can make up new messages in code for their partner to do.
- Some might need to have a sheet with the FL and the figures to refer to for this and for the next activity.

DECIPHERING AND CRACKING THE CODE USING NUMBERS

Preparation

- Here, all the letters in the text are represented by numbers, as above, but you only give a few to the students.
- Make sure that the few you give occur frequently and that students can get one or two words from them.

Activity

- The students decipher the message as far as they can with the numbers you have given and **then deduce the numbers** for the other letters, hence cracking the code as well as deciphering the message. This puts more emphasis on spelling and remembering words.

(Thanks to Barbara Bettsworth, for this.)

MISSING VOWELS

Create a list of words where all the vowels are missing. Students can have access to an *aide-mémoire* if they choose. Or put a code in instead of each vowel with a key for reference.

▮ Missing consonants

As above, but create a list of words where certain consonants are missing.

▮ Anagrams for words

Preparation

• Write the anagrams on the board or have them on the OHP.

Activity

• Students work out the words or sentences and then copy up into their books.

For support, prepare the anagrams on card, allowing the students to cut up the letters, so that they can physically arrange them, or give them out in envelopes already cut up.

As further support for students with reading difficulties, you can help by cutting the cards in irregular ways, so that the letters are joined like a jigsaw. These cards could then be stuck into the students' files or copied out.

As further support for students with writing difficulties, you may need to make a special set of cards for any student who has problems forming letters. These cards could contain the letters written very faintly (use a stencil font on the computer), so that the student can put the cards in the right order, write over the letter forms in felt-tip and stick them in his or her book.

▮ Sentence puzzles

As above, except that the cards contain words that form a sentence.

You could use the same strategies as above to help students with reading difficulties and you could colour-code words. For example, if there are three sentences in the puzzle, the set of words for each sentence is in a different colour – if you are using word-processed sheets, you could also use different fonts instead of different colours.

▮ Grid codes

When getting students to generate language for revision purposes, for example on what we can do around town, we can categorise the language into a 'structures' grid (see example below), then exploit this further.

Preparation

• Number all the items in the grid.

Activity

- Prepare a sheet with mini-dialogues, all represented by numbers and letters.
- The students find the numbers on the grid and write out the mini-dialogues, with letters A and B representing the two partners.

Early finishers make up some coded dialogues for others.

Structures grid

Mini-dialogues

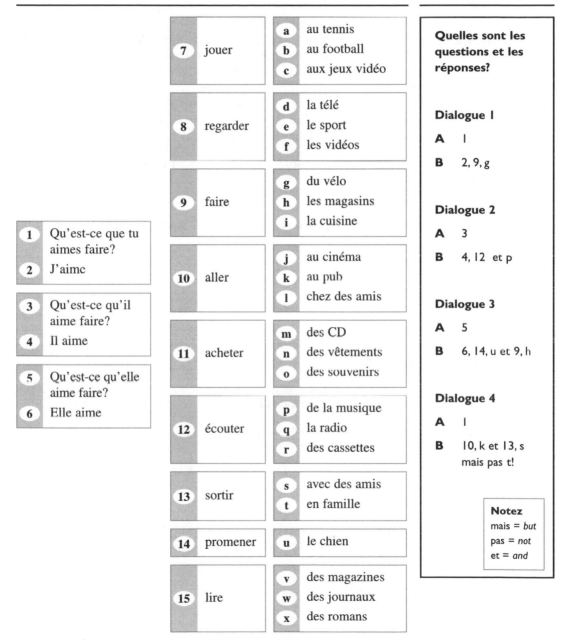

7	jouer	**a**	au tennis
		b	au football
		c	aux jeux vidéo
8	regarder	**d**	la télé
		e	le sport
		f	les vidéos
9	faire	**g**	du vélo
		h	les magasins
		i	la cuisine
10	aller	**j**	au cinéma
		k	au pub
		l	chez des amis
11	acheter	**m**	des CD
		n	des vêtements
		o	des souvenirs
12	écouter	**p**	de la musique
		q	la radio
		r	des cassettes
13	sortir	**s**	avec des amis
		t	en famille
14	promener	**u**	le chien
15	lire	**v**	des magazines
		w	des journaux
		x	des romans

1	Qu'est-ce que tu aimes faire?
2	J'aime
3	Qu'est-ce qu'il aime faire?
4	Il aime
5	Qu'est-ce qu'elle aime faire?
6	Elle aime

Quelles sont les questions et les réponses?

Dialogue 1

A   1

B   2, 9, g

Dialogue 2

A   3

B   4, 12 et p

Dialogue 3

A   5

B   6, 14, u et 9, h

Dialogue 4

A   1

B   10, k et 13, s mais pas t!

Notez
mais = *but*
pas = *not*
et = *and*

9 Creating a logical sequence of activities in lesson planning

Creating a series of activities that lead logically into one another helps classes to see where they are heading. (For another example of this, see Part 2: *Yes – but will they behave?*, Chapter 3. See also *Reflections on motivation*, Chapter 6, p77, where Jim McElwee gives an example of logical progression using ICT.) In the three examples below, activities from earlier chapters have been chosen, to show how we can take lessons through logical stages towards an open-ended activity, which allows the students to choose from the language they have learned to produce something of their own creation.

How we can include all students and differentiate for them in the open-ended activities is illustrated in Chapter 3.

 ## GIVING INFORMATION ABOUT THE TOWN AND SURROUNDING AREA

Presentation

Language is generated by the class and linked into what the teacher has prepared for that lesson (see p30).

Language recognition

Telepathy (see p39). The OHT would contain pictures of leisure activities and the dialogue accompanying the activity would be as follows:

Class	*Qu'est-ce qu'on peut faire ici?*
Teacher	*On peut aller au cinéma?*
Student	*Oui, c'est possible* or *Non, je regrette* (according to how the teacher points).

Repetition

- Students repeat the question and structures for the responses using rhythm.
- Places to visit are repeated through the song, ''Ere we go'.

Practice

- **Listening and Speaking:** Win the card (see p47).
- **Writing:** Grid codes (see p54).
- **Open-ended activity:** posters or leaflets including all language generated at the beginning.

DATES AND BIRTHDAYS

Presentation

Students make cards with their names on one side and their birthday on the other and the class and teacher record these (see p32).

Language recognition

Grab-a-card using the cards they have made (see p38).

Repetition

- Numbers to mimes thought up by the class (see p44).
- Months to chants and rhythms (see p41).

Practice

- **Writing:** each student chooses six people in the class and uses the birthday list and the grid on the right to write down the dates in words.

- **Speaking:** students teach and test each other in pairs (see p51).

Student's book

- Open-ended activity: students use recycled language to describe a teacher, giving his or her birthday and making a list of presents he or she would like – photos could accompany the display.

C'est quand? C'est le ...			
1st	premier	17th	dix-sept
2nd	deux	18th	dix-huit
3rd	trois	19th	dix-neuf
4th	quatre	20th	vingt
5th	cinq	21st	vingt et un
6th	six	22nd	vingt-deux
7th	sept	23rd	vingt-trois
8th	huit	24th	vingt-quatre
9th	neuf	25th	vingt-cinq
10th	dix	26th	vingt-six
11th	onze	27th	vingt-sept
12th	douze	28th	vingt-huit
13th	treize	29th	vingt-neuf
14th	quatorze	30th	trente
15th	quinze	31st	trente et un
16th	seize		

janvier	février	mars
avril	mai	juin
juillet	août	septembre
octobre	novembre	décembre

PERSONALITIES

Presentation and repetition

Students make cards with names of well-known people and stick them on the white board (see p33). The teacher gets the class to repeat more difficult words during the presentation stage using 'forwards and backwards' or rhythm.

Language recognition: championships

- One volunteer comes to the front.
- The volunteer chooses an opponent.
- The teacher covers up the English.
- The teacher gives a characteristic in the FL.
- The first student to give the correct English is now the champion and chooses the next adversary.

Practice

- **Listening and Speaking:** students teach and test each other with their own grid. See pp51–52.
- **Writing:** students complete a worksheet (see *Arbeitsblatt* opposite) which gradually gets them to elaborate and then to write sentences independently. This was particularly successful with a Year 9 lower set. One student who normally did nothing at all produced an excellent sentence at the end: *Cindy Crawford ist attraktiv aber sehr doof.* Another student deeply in love with a boy in the class wrote: *Jonny ist sehr, sehr, sehr, sehr, sehr, sehr, sehr, sehr, sehr, sehr, sehr, sehr, sehr, sehr, sehr, sehr, schön.* Well, it was a long sentence!
- **Open-ended activity:** students choose one of their sentences and use A4 paper to create a drawing and subtitle to contribute towards a classroom display. Here are some examples of posters:

ARBEITSBLATT

A

I		ist	beliebt
2		ist	nervös
3	Ross	ist	
4	Herr Smith		
5			

B

...*er als* = more than

I		ist	lustiger	als	
2		ist	attraktiver	als	
3		ist	faul___	als	
4	Frau Alison	ist	_____er	als	
5	Katie				

C

aber = but

I	Cindy Crawford	ist	attraktiv	aber	
2	Frau Jones	ist	nett		
3		ist	beliebt		

D

ziemlich = rather   *sehr* = very

I		ist	ziemlich	lustig
2		ist	sehr	
3		ist		
4				

E   Mach deine eigene Sätze und ein Bild in deinem Heft.

Conclusion

This is all very well, some may say, but what if a class just will not repeat language, do pairwork, talk, be quiet, listen, in fact do anything at all? What if, in spite of everything we do they are just not bothered?

I experienced this myself, while working with a Year 9 lower set alongside a teacher new to his school. I also worked with other teachers in a similar position. Indeed, it is a real problem when students disregard everything we try to do. Between us, we found that the best way to tackle total inattention was to avoid at all costs having to speak to the class as a whole group. In order to get them to notice us, we need to break down the barriers they are setting up. This means getting to know them individually, which necessitates giving them something to do which interests them so that we can circulate and talk to individuals. The best way to demonstrate how this is possible is to give two examples, both involving Year 9 lower sets and teachers new to their school.

Example I

This class had had a patchy history of language learning and they had retained hardly anything at all. How could we give them something to do without teaching them first and without instructions? We decided that the priority was to get them quieter because, as they were, they wouldn't learn anything anyway. What could we give them to do that they would want to do? We picked something that would allow them to talk about their own dreams and to be creative. We decided that over several lessons they could make a booklet of their ideal life, consisting of pictures and captions. In the first lesson, they drew a house of their dreams (see opposite) and wrote something about it. In the following lessons they added a family of their dreams, a school of their dreams, etc. This allowed them to use any language retained from earlier learning, although they relied heavily on us for help. This was a good way of getting round to them and talking with them about personal things. Gradually, it was possible to introduce more interactive tasks.

A dream house

Example 2

Another class had the same patchy history and the topic they were to work on was 'Holidays'. We decided to get them to make 'list posters'. The next lesson the question, *'Où es-tu allé en vacances?'* (Where did you go on holiday?), with a choice of replies, was put on the board. The students worked on a piece of A4 paper in landscape, and wrote the question and an answer of their choice below in large letters with felt-tips. On the other side they illustrated it. The next lesson the question, *'Avec qui es tu allé en vacances?'* (Who did you go on holiday with?), with, again, a choice of replies was put on the board. On a new piece of paper they wrote the question and an answer of their choice below in large letters with felt-tips. They then sellotaped this piece of paper to the one from the lesson before. They progressed in this way over five or six lessons, creating a long dialogue one side and pictures the other, which they could use to teach and test one another.

The important factor in both examples, is that we were not just trying to 'contain' them by worksheet. We attempted to include the basic ingredients for motivation in this book. Students had the opportunity to express their personal thoughts and ideas, and the task was open-ended and manageable. They also had an on-going purpose, to complete a booklet for others to read and a strip poster to use in pair work. Because of this, they got on with it, and their teachers were able to gradually move them on to the kinds of activities and lessons illustrated in this book.

Bibliography

Calvert, M. and Chambers, G. (eds) (2001) Reflections on Practice 6: *Reflections on motivation.* CILT.

Harris V., Burch J., Jones, B. and Darcy, J. (2001) *Something to say? Promoting spontaneous classroom talk.* CILT.

Jones, B. and Jones, G. (2001) *Boys' performance in Modern Foreign Languages: listening to learners.* CILT.

Department for Education and Employment and QCA (1999) *The National Curriculum for England: Modern Foreign Languages Key Stages 3 and 4.*

Further reading

Convery, A. and Coyle, D. (1999) Pathfinder 37: *Differentiation and individual learners: a guide for classroom practice.* CILT.

Harris, V. 'Making boys make progress'. *Language Learning Journal,* 18: 56–62.

Phipps, W. (1999) Pathfinder 38: *Pairwork: interaction in the Modern Languages classroom.* CILT.

Part 2

Yes — but will they behave?

Managing the interactive classroom

Susan Halliwell

Introduction

I can't possibly do pairwork with that group, they won't stop talking to each other!'

There is a very narrow line between liveliness and restlessness. As we develop more interactive styles of language teaching which encourage plenty of oral work, simultaneous pairwork, movement around the room and scope for the pupils' sense of fun and imagination, we are all faced with the question of how to organise events so that the liveliness works **for** learning not against it. Some teachers will be able to rely on their personality and their established authority to carry them through whatever teaching method they adopt. Others will develop a teaching style which moves away from the centrally imposed control of the teacher and sets up more independent learning. Most of us, however, will encounter somewhere in our teaching the kind of restlessness and unco-operativeness which can make any form of foreign language work seem an uphill task and can make oral work, in particular, seem dispiritingly unrealistic. Under those circumstances, it is very tempting to abandon exactly the kind of interactive teaching which in less pressured moments we are quite happy to agree is exactly what the pupils both want and need. Even with basically willing and co-operative classes, language lessons can seem hard work and can border on the frenetic.

The question then is how to organise language lessons so that they offer opportunities for real communication and lively interaction while maintaining a reasonable working atmosphere for pupils and teachers alike.

The starting point of this part of the book is simple and is something that teachers know instinctively. We all know that, quite independently of the teacher, some activities calm a class down and others stir them up. By exploring this very simple fact in greater depth and by developing quite deliberate strategies based on the insights it offers, the book suggests how, without losing sight of our ideals:

• we can avoid creating problems unnecessarily;
• we can respond constructively to problems which nonetheless do arise;
• we can reduce, even in a more interactive classroom, the need for the kind of overtly imposed control which demands more energy, will power and charismatic personality than most of us have.

The suggestions here apply whether you are teaching from a coursebook or from your own materials and whether you have basically amenable classes or the kind which only have to be mentioned in the staffroom to produce an almost Pavlovian chorus of groans! The ideas offered are not the only approach to the question of interactive language work and control, nor will they solve everything, but they have helped me and have helped those I have already shared them with. I hope they will help you.

1 Anticipating the effect of an activity

Most of us have heard ourselves say at some time the equivalent of 'OK, if you can't do this sensibly [it's usually something we've spent literally hours preparing!] then we'll have to do something really boring. So get out your exercise books ...'

We can take this instinctive response and awareness further. We can **anticipate** the probable effects of certain classroom activities and quite deliberately use that insight to construct a controlled framework for an interactive lesson. There are two key questions, which are interrelated:

• Does the activity stir or does it settle?
• In what way does it involve the learner?

DOES IT STIR OR DOES IT SETTLE?

The terms 'stir' and 'settle' are not intended to carry any overtones of good or bad. 'Stir' can be positive in the sense of waking a class up or it can be negative in the sense of making them restless. 'Settle', similarly, can mean that a class calms down or it can mean that they sink into a kind of stupefied boredom.

Exactly what you personally find stirs or settles your classes is a matter of your individual experience, circumstances and style. However, within the variations there is a core of experience common to most of us. If we look at the four skills, for example, most of us will agree that as a general rule oral work stirs, listening and reading usually settle and on most occasions writing settles a class like magic. The type of activity within those skills also makes a difference. So games and competitions, for example, tend to stir. Mechanical routines on the other hand tend to settle.

It helps to make yourself lists like those started on the next page. In the particular lists here activities are described in rather general categories. More specific examples are only noted in brackets. This is because my personal set of teaching activities and the shorthand labels I have for them would not necessarily mean anything to anyone else. However, when you make your own list it is a good idea to be as specific as you can.

You can apply the stir/settle distinction to any typical or regular features of your teaching. Do you, for example, have a set of questions and answers with which you routinely begin lessons? If so, ask yourself whether the classes are more settled or more stirred at the end of the routine than they were at the beginning.

teacher/pupil oral work (question/
answer, checking exercises,
repetition etc)

competitions (blackboard 'oxo', lotto,
find me a ..., team games etc)

games (guess what I've got on my
flashcard / in my hand / on OHP,
battleships, pelmanism reading
game etc)

pupil/pupil oral work (dialogues,
sondages, drills etc)

acting
pair-work ... ?
just listening ... ?

- - - -
- - - -

Activities which usually stir

Activities which usually settle

copying (particularly from a book)
drawing / labelling / colouring
listening WITH SOMETHING TO DO
(grids, tick which one you hear,
find the word, arrange the
sequence, draw what I
describe etc)

being read to / being told a story
watching a video
reading alone
some pair-work ... ?

- - - -
- - - -

In fact, in reading the above lists, or in writing your own and perhaps discussing them with other teachers, you will already have discovered that there is not a tidy distinction between the two categories. You will probably have found yourself thinking something like 'X works as a settler, but only if ...' or 'Yes, but sometimes ...'. There is obviously another factor at work. Pairwork shows this particularly well. It can lead to noisy inattentive classes or it can lead to classes which are still fairly noisy but in a busy absorbed way. What makes the difference is the degree and nature of involvement which the activity demands or offers.

HOW DOES THE ACTIVITY INVOLVE THE LEARNERS?

We can distinguish, although not separate completely, those activities which engage the emotions or the mind and those which occupy the learners physically.

Mental engagement

Games, for example, engage the learners' minds by appealing to their sense of fun or their appetite for competition. So, for different reasons, do things they have to work out, like logic puzzles or codes.

Their minds are also engaged when they are teasing their friends, expressing their sense of humour or using their imagination. In a describe-and-arrange activity, for example, when one partner has to find out without looking how the other has arranged a set of furniture items on a base picture of a house, it is fairly common for learners to attempt to confuse their friends deliberately by doing something offbeat like putting the fridge in the bathroom …

… or as one character wrote in a 'note for the electrician: '… *la clef est sous le chien*'!

At an older level, a sixth-form class will get quite involved generating a story to 'explain' a picture like the one here.

We probably see the truest form of mental engagement when a class is learning something else through the medium of the language they are learning, say 'doing Science' in Russian.

This kind of mental engagement is one of the ways in which learners make the language event their own and are not just mouthing others' routines or sentiments. So, the more the better. However, on its own it is often not enough to keep a class working effectively.

Physical occupation

Other activities give learners something physical to do. At one level, speaking is itself a kind of physical involvement in events. Writing is even more obviously occupying. This is often just 'paper-and-pencil work' of some kind. It might just be copying or, if the class is younger, drawing and colouring. Sometimes the physical activity may be as a result of listening. For example, perhaps pupils have to check items off a list as they hear them or follow a route round a map as they listen to directions (again!). Alternatively, they may be completing a grid with the information they hear. More interestingly, they could be making something by following either spoken or written instructions. They can draw a picture someone else describes. They can make something origami fashion. They can arrange objects or construct something according to instructions. There are also those activities like 'Simon says' which demand rapid physical response. There are others which occupy the learners actively by requiring them to get up and move round the room. One personal favourite is a poster search. For this they have to collect information from a series of 'posters' round the walls. Various forms of class survey or *sondages* also involve movement around the room. Or there are activities in which they are each given a card and by asking questions (not looking!) have to find the other person in the room who has an identical card to theirs.

INVOLVEMENT AND BEHAVIOUR

Both of these forms of involvement, that is both physical and mental involvement, contribute positively to the behaviour in an interactive lesson, but each on its own has its limitations which can add to our potential difficulties if they are not taken into account. For example, we need to remind ourselves that excitement with nothing physically active to do can create problems of restlessness. Team games seem like a good idea. But team games which only actively involve one participant from each team at a time and rely on mental involvement alone to hold the attention of the others, often end with rather silly and disruptive arguments about the fairness or otherwise of the scoring system. So we would be looking for ways of retaining the fun but calming things down by giving all the participants something to do. Equally, however physically occupying an activity is, if the work is intellectually and emotionally empty it can lead to boredom. Repeating learnt dialogues in pairs, for example, theoretically occupies everyone and we might expect the activity to be settling. But precisely because they are merely repeating something learnt rather than thinking for themselves or expressing themselves, it doesn't offer the mind or the soul much and the pupils tend to look for other distractions!

On the other hand, look at an activity which you might have expected to make for problems. In the 'poster search' just mentioned, the class moves round the room looking for information on posters on the walls. This is exactly the kind of activity we might be wary of with a difficult class. In fact, it works because it combines mental and physical involvement. It works precisely because they **are** able to move about, talk to each other **and** usually enjoy the challenge of spotting the answer (one Year 10 group surprised me by calling it a treasure hunt). They get on with it. There will be noise and normal adolescent shuffle, but the class will be working.

If we know all this, we can look for ways of adjusting the activities to suit the mood of a lesson.

Adjusting the activities

Once you start thinking along these lines, you will find that there is often more than one version of an activity which can provide the same linguistic experience while creating a different kind of mood in the room.

TURNING A STIRRER INTO A SETTLER

Suppose, for example, you have a list of vocabulary for food and drink which you want to revise. You are still at the stage of getting the class to recognise the vocabulary. So you decide to do it in some form of 'Lotto'. The advantage of this is that it gives a meaningful purpose to the act of repetitive recognition by turning it into a game.

However, although it is a 'paper-and-pencil' activity which physically occupies the whole class at the same time, it is a highly competitive game that generates excitement and tension. In other words, it can prove something of a stirrer. That is no problem in itself: you may want to wake the class up. On the other hand, if for whatever reasons the class needs calming down then you may well want to set up something more settling. At the same time, you don't want to have to abandon this bit of the lesson altogether.

One possibility is to turn it into a simple write-down-the-number-of-the-word-I-say activity. The linguistic practice provided is just the same, but the exercise has a different effect on the mood of the class. It could go like this:

A settling version of vocabulary revision

- Write your words/stick your flashcards/draw your symbols on the board and number them (you may even find the items are already numbered in the coursebook, in which case you can just work from the book).

1 [   ]
2 [   ]
3 [   ]
4 [   ]
5 [   ]

- Quickly run through the list, saying the word or phrase represented by each prompt.

- Now say the words/phrases in random order. The class has to write down the numbers in the order you refer to them.

- Repeat this as many times as you like, just varying the order. (If you have a lot of words, you may find it works better to do several blocks of five or six at a time rather than all in one go.)

Another possible settling version of the same linguistic activity as Lotto is the familiar grid to complete.

If you do not have one ready, you could build up an instant on-the-spot grid on the board. (I personally prefer the class to do this kind of work on scrap paper – then they do not have to spend so long making the grid neat or drawing beautifully. It also avoids filling up their exercise books with meaningless lists of ticks and crosses or numbers, etc.) Notice that in spite of the change of outer form, the underlying linguistic task remains the same. Remember, too, that because you are using this as a settler you need to set it up as swiftly and as uncomplicatedly as possible. One way to do it might be as follows:

On the spot grid

- Write the words or initial letters/draw the symbols (keep it simple)/stick five or six prompts across the board, drawing in the vertical lines as you go (the class can start copying as soon as you start; the copying is itself settling).

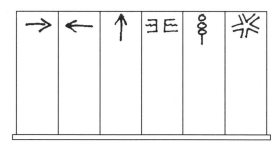

- Start writing/drawing the first prompts in the left-hand column.

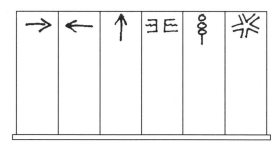

- As soon as you can see that the majority of the class has the first prompt in place, read out your first statement and mark the information on the board grid as they complete theirs. This helps to establish what is happening.

Pour aller à la banque, continuez tout droit puis traversez le pont.

- Continue with further statements. It is interesting that words and phrases themselves can contribute to stir/settle. Here, since the intention is to settle the class, we can stick to the rather boringly predictable camping site, etc. But on other occasions why not stir things up a bit with a visit to the sewers (a genuine part of the Paris tourist scene), or a stick insect in the list of pets?

→	←	↑	彐E	⚇	⁂
B		1	2		
H	1	3		2	
C					

Finally, I personally have a standby settler sheet (see overleaf) which feels like a test (mega-settler!), but it too makes the same linguistic demands and offers the same linguistic practice as Lotto. It also has the advantage that it can be used with any phrase or word, simple or complex, provided you have set up some way of referring to them by numbers.

I use as many of the boxes as I need to settle the class down initially with series of a write-down-the-number-of-the-one-you-hear. Meanwhile, I decide what I am going to use the rest of the space for! If the going is still tough I will probably use it for another writing activity (maybe an instant grid, maybe copying and label, maybe an exercise from the book), or if things have got better I shall try to use it for something a bit more interesting but still settling.

These particular examples may not appeal to you, but what matters is that we each find ways of giving ourselves room for manoeuvre.

NAME _____

a _____

b _____

c _____

d _____

e _____

f _____

a _____

b _____

c _____

d _____

e _____

f _____

a _____

b _____

c _____

d _____

e _____

f _____

a _____

b _____

c _____

d _____

e _____

f _____

a _____

b _____

c _____

d _____

e _____

f _____

a _____

b _____

c _____

d _____

e _____

f _____

A similar kind of adjustment is possible in matters of involvement. Obviously, the best activities are those which involve pupils both actively and mentally, for example fitting these strips of jumbled sentence halves together.

Notice that we have the advantage over the book here in that we can actually give the class pieces of paper to move around. The exercise is much duller on the printed page.

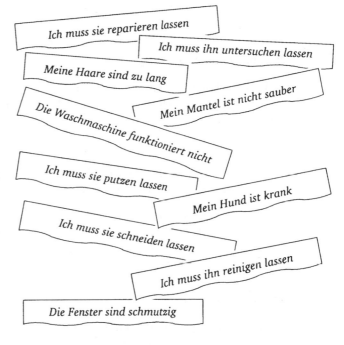

In ways like these you can look for adaptations to increase the mental engagement of mentally involving activities. Writing about these things makes them sound rather heavy-going and complicated. They don't need to be. Here are two examples to give you the general idea.

INCREASING ACTUAL OCCUPATION

There are various versions of the activity which involves the class guessing which phrase/word/object one of their classmates has chosen. In the usual version, one pupil selects a flashcard or a word/phrase from a list and the others guess.

> *¿Vas al banco?*
> *No.*
> *¿Vas al correo?*
> *No.*
> *¿Vas al supermercado?*
> *Si – si voy.*

A more complicated version further up the school might go: '*Wenn das Wetter schöner gewesen wäre, hättest du ...?*'

This can keep even a large class fairly happy for some time because it is fun and it makes them think. Even so, there are disadvantages to the activity in this form. Firstly, any single pupil, even if willing to speak, is not going to have more than one or two chances to do so. Secondly, only one learner is actually speaking at a time. So in this form the activity is mentally engaging but does not involve enough of the class activity. It is therefore a good idea, once it is clear what they have to do, to turn the activity into pairwork in some way. It could go like this:

Paired guessing

- Write/stick/draw prompts on board and number them. Pupil A in each pair writes down the number of the destination he or she has chosen.

- Partner B starts to guess: ¿ *Vas al supermercado?*, etc.

- When B has guessed A's choice correctly they change over. B chooses a destination and A has to guess.

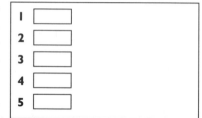

In this way, you have added actual involvement to the mental involvement of the original. In fact, at a later stage, once they are handling the oral work well and you want to move on to writing, you can turn this into an even more physically involving activity without losing the mental engagement of guessing.

Written guessing

- The prompts are on the board and numbered for reference as before. (You may also want to have the written form up. The bright ones don't refer to it, the middle ones will occasionally check and it provides a constant reminder for those who need it.)

- Both partners choose a phrase. (If they don't trust each other they can write down the 'reference number' of the phrase somewhere out of sight.) Each then has to guess what the other's phrase is.

- Each partner writes a first guess in the form of a question and they swap papers.

¿ Vas al correo ?

A's paper

¿ Vas al banco ?

B's paper

- They indicate on the paper whether their opponent's guess was correct and swap papers back.

¿ Vás al correo ?
¡ No!
¿ Vas al banco?
Si, si voy.

¿ Vas al banco?
¡ No!
¿ Vas al supermercado?
¡No!

- They each write the next question and carry on like this until one of them has guessed correctly and scored a point.

- They choose again and start again keeping a score as they go.

So much for increasing actual occupation. In the same way, you can increase the mental engagement in something which is effectively occupying but otherwise easily becomes mindless.

INCREASING MENTAL ENGAGEMENT

For example, suppose you want a class to get various words connected with shops and shopping into their books. They can, of course, just copy out the list from their coursebook or the board. There will be times when that is all you want to do. But we want the list in their heads as well as in their books. Writing the word just once does not provide much practice and it is possible to copy out lists of words without thinking very much about their meaning. You could increase the mental engagement and the chances of effective learning by asking the class to list their words in categories like this:

im Wohnzimmer   im Schlafzimmer

    der Tisch   *der Schrank*

    der Stuhl   *der Fernseher*

    die Lampe

in der Küche   im Badezimmer

    der Tisch

    der Stuhl

    die Lampe

If this idea appeals to you, there are several ways you can turn it into a much fuller version. Here is one:

Listing

- Ask the class to work in pairs to make a rough list of any weather phrases they know – they can approximate if they don't know how to spell them. Give them a couple of minutes to do this.

- On one side of the board or on the OHP collect together the phrases they have thought of. (This is your chance to spell their rough or half-remembered versions correctly. At this stage, I prefer just to let them tell me, in however rough and ready form, what they have thought of. I do not ask them to spell the phrases. After all, if they can already produce all these in correct spelling, there is no need to do the activity!)

- When you have collected a reasonable list on the board or the OHP, read them through quickly with the class so they are reminded of the sound before they write them.

- Next write the four seasons up as headings.

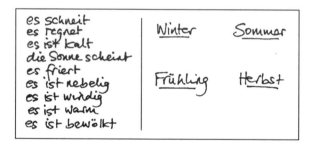

- Read out one of the phrases and allocate it to a season. (Choose one which will make it clear that things can come in more than one category.)

- Do a couple of examples like this and then set the class to write the column headings in their own books and to make the lists according to what they think is appropriate.

There are plenty of categories and items you can use this technique with, e.g. shops and purchases, weather and clothes, days of the week and school subjects, rooms and furniture and so on. The only thing to remember is that you want to provide personal choice but you also want the items to come up several times (or as one of my pupils said perceptively, though not eloquently, to his neighbour 'I've just written *es* bloody *regnet* four times!').

SO WHAT!

To say all this may seem to be labouring the point and stating the obvious. It may well be obvious, but even so it is not uncommon for the start of a long lesson or the whole of a short lesson to follow a pattern something like this:

Aim: to practise request + food		
Time	**Activity**	**Comment**
5 mins	General questions routine	Oral, one pupil at a time – STIR
5 mins	Revision of food vocabulary flashcards and repetition	Oral, little occupation or mental involvement, therefore STIR
5 mins	Practise request and food with exercise p120	Oral, little occupation or mental involvement, therefore STIR
5 mins	Practise reading dialogue p121	Oral/reading, a bit more occupation but still little mental involvement, therefore STIR
10 mins	In pairs practise dialogue p121 ready for acting out	

I have exaggerated this slightly to make the point, but set out in this way it becomes clear that the first twenty minutes or so of a lesson like this would offer little to settle or to occupy the bulk of the class, so that by the time the teacher came to set up the interactive work the class would at best be probably only partly attentive and willing. If this were the beginning of a double period, the situation could become even more uncomfortable. Even with a fairly ordinary class and a short single period, the lesson as it stands could prove quite a handful. There would certainly be problems ahead if the class contained a sizeable proportion of the uncommitted or easily distracted.

Obviously some teachers can assert control, but why set up a lesson so that we constantly have to? Our understanding of stir/settle and involvement doesn't just give us flexibility in the form of the activities themselves, it also gives us flexibility in respect of the way in which we can sequence activities and have some control over the general mood of the lesson.

3 Adjusting the sequence of activities

There are perhaps three main ways in which we can usefully adjust lessons taking stir/settle and the contributory factor of involvement into account.

- We can start lessons in such a way as to calm a class down.
- We can try to make sure that lively work starts from and returns to a relatively calm base.
- We are in a better position to handle those lessons which are longer than we would ideally have chosen.

 ## STARTING LESSONS CALMLY

Unless you have the kind of class you have to kick-start in order to achieve anything at all, it helps to begin most lessons with something calming. We all have ways of settling classes down right at the beginning before we start work. But there is no point in throwing away that hard-won attention by then making the first twenty minutes of activities stirring or not very involving. So one technique is quite deliberately to insert settlers at the beginning of the lesson. In fact, if you find you can't get quiet by demanding it or if you prefer a more indirect control, then these activities will often help slide a class into a calm mood.

What settlers people use are a matter of personal preference. Here are three possibilities. The first is based on writing, the second on listening and the third on reading. They are all quite deliberately **very** basic. If they take time to set up or if they are complicated they no longer work as settlers.

Suggestion 1	Get the class to copy a brief list of words/phrases/structures which you are going to focus on later.
Suggestion 2	Try the write-down-the-number-of-the-one-I-say activity set out on page 71.
Suggestion 3	Get the class to turn to the page in the book which you are going to use later. Read out in random order a collection of key words/phrases/structures which occur in the text. The class has to track them down in the text and copy them out.

These settling tasks may be very basic but they are not pointless. They can be a way to highlight the focus of the lesson or to ease the way into a rather large chunk of text.

Remember, too, that these settlers can be combined to provide a more prolonged calming start on those occasions when the class has come into the room with their hair standing up on end. This leads us on to the question of longer sequences of activities and particularly those leading up to and following interactive work of some kind.

PROVIDING A CALM CONTEXT FOR LIVELY WORK

We can't ask young people to have fun, move about, talk to each other, etc and then be surprised and annoyed if they get noisy and excited.

'You are to practise this dialogue in pairs – and there is to be no talking!'

So, if we know that something lively is coming up, we can sandwich it between activities which are basically calming. For example, suppose you are planning to get the class to learn some dialogues, practise them in pairs and then 'act' them out in front of the others. For reasons already discussed, the practising of the dialogues often won't hold their attention for long enough for them to learn the dialogues! And because watching or listening to your classmates isn't very involving, many classes are not very good at keeping quiet while others are doing their bit. So you can set up the mood more calmly by making sure that the pairwork follows and is followed by settlers rather than stirrers. For example:

* in pairs, arrange the dialogue on strips of paper into the right sequence (or a possible sequence; no reason why everyone should have to do your thing);
* practise it in pairs and do some acting out;
* each pair copies up its chosen version.

For more difficult situations, you can make this interweaving of stir and settle more frequent. For example, a more extreme version might then look like this:

* paired rehearsing of dialogues, as planned;
* switch to a sort-the-strips-into-order activity based on the dialogue;
* bit more dialogue repeating;
* then some acting out, as planned;
* then copy out the strip dialogue they have previously sorted out;
* then back to a couple more acting out. If you still want to continue with the dialogue but the pronunciation is going to pot, you can combine a reminder of what it sounds like with a settler in the form of some version of write-down-the-number-of-the-one-you-hear;
* final return to acting out dialogues.

This kind of interweaving of stir and settle is also what makes long lessons much more manageable.

PACING LONG LESSONS

We seem, at times, to have got into the way of thinking of good language teaching as resembling some kind of song-and-dance routine. 'Superteach' bounds confidently into the classroom with a song at the ready, paper bag puppets in the left hand, flashcards in the right, a stick of chalk between the teeth and a chin operated tape-recorder slung round the neck!

'Right! Calm down!'

We are asking the impossible of ourselves if we try to teach at maximum pitch all the time. More importantly, we are letting the learners down. They need peace and quiet in their lives as well as stimulation and excitement. Schools may be one of the few remaining places where some of them have a chance of finding it. We cannot moan about their inability to concentrate if we subject them to a constant barrage of high voltage activities. Besides, our language lesson is only one in their day's programme. So we owe them – and need for our own sake – periods of calm among the bursts of activity.

To oversimplify again, you can use the stir/settle concept to create a pattern a bit like this:

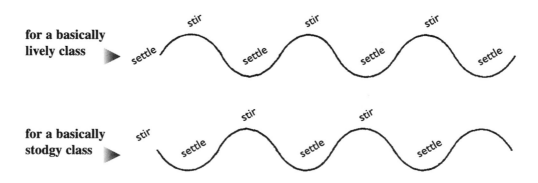

This kind of planning isn't a long and complicated process. Once you've decided to think in this way it becomes almost instinctive. It also works! By varying the mood in this way through the choice and sequence of activities we have more chance of making sure that a long lesson does not build up unstoppably to a pitch of unacceptable behaviour or slide down into a slough of dullness.

It may help to summarise all these points if we return to the lesson on requests + food on p79. Here is an alternative version which puts some of the suggestions in this book into practice.

Aim: to practise request + food

Time	Activity	Comment
15 mins	On arrival, class to copy food list onto rough paper/rough books/back of books	Simultaneously occupying, SETTLER
	With flashcards numbered on board do 'write down the number of the one you hear'.	Simultaneously occupying with a little more mental engagement, but still SETTLING
	(approx. 3 times + vary it to true/false, i.e. 1 des frites – vrai? faux?)	
10 mins	Practise questions with 'guess what I've got on my flashcard'.	STIR, mentally engaging
	Paired 'guess what I've got on my flashcard'.	STIR, mentally engaging + simultaneously **occupying**
	Write vous désirez on board.	
5 mins	'Dictation', i.e. recognition and copying of request + food (front of books as record).	RESETTLE with simultaneous occupation (writing) + mental engagement in order to remind of sound and settle before STIR
	In pairs, practise dialogue p121 ready for acting out	

Conclusion

It is very tempting with difficult classes to set up lessons which are all settlers. (Or as one eleven year-old once assured me on transferring to secondary school 'I don't do French … I draw'.) That defeats the purpose of the exercise which is to calm things down sometimes, so that at other times you can do more lively things without events getting out of hand.

This isn't just a negative mechanism for dealing with energetic classes, though the focus in this part of the book has been on control. The approach is just as valid as a way of making sure that we wake up our more plodding classes.

Finally, there are conventions about language teaching which imply that some activities are inherently **good** and others are inherently **bad.** For example, teachers can be made to feel very guilty about asking their class to copy or getting them to write words before they have said them. I am not dismissing those conventions. They are based on helpful pedagogic insights. I am arguing, however, that no single activity or sequence of activities is **good** if it causes problems in terms of the human reactions to the lessons. A flower is a weed if there are too many of them or they are in the wrong place. For our own sanity and the sake of our classes, we have to take people as well as more theoretical language pedagogy into account.

timeless topics for all MFL teachers

Classic Pathfinders

deal with those MFL issues that will never go away. Based on the wisdom contained in the best-selling titles in the series, the material has been re-written and updated by the original authors in the light of the challenges of today's classroom. Each title contains re-editions of two related titles in the *Pathfinder* range which are truly 'classic'.

Classic Pathfinders are for:

- experienced teachers refreshing or renewing their practice – particularly as they go into positions of leadership and need to articulate the principles of good practice;
- newly qualified or beginner teachers who want to build up the essentials of good language-teaching methodology.

Classic Pathfinder 1

You speak, they speak: focus on target language use

Bernardette Holmes, Barry Jones and Susan Halliwell

.This book is based on two of CILT's earliest and most influential *Pathfinders*. It shows how it is possible develop an ethos of communication in the target language involving teacher to pupil, pupil to teacher, and pupil to pupil interaction.

The material has been updated and re-written, where appropriate, to take account of current curriculum initiatives and research.

classic pathfinder

new pathfinder

New Pathfinders

provide an expert MFL perspective on national initiatives. They are designed to support the language-teaching profession by ensuring that MFL has its own voice and ideas on the issues in education today.

New Pathfinders provide user-friendly support, advice and reference material for today's CPD agenda.

New Pathfinder 1

Raising the standard: addressing the needs of gifted and talented pupils

Anneli McLachlan

The author presents a strategic approach to tapping the potential of high-ability pupils. She shows how re-analysing teaching and learning styles to cater for the most able can help raise the standard of all learners.

'Pathfinders *get better and better. This* Pathfinder *is excellent'*

Jane Jones, Head of MFL Teacher Education, King's College London

New Pathfinder 2

The language of success: improving grades at GCSE

Dave Carter

This book presents strategies to help all students achieve their best possible grade at GCSE.